Human Geography: A Very Short Introduction

VERY SHORT INTRODUCTIONS are for anyone wanting a stimulating and accessible way into a new subject. They are written by experts, and have been translated into more than 45 different languages.

The series began in 1995, and now covers a wide variety of topics in every discipline. The VSI library currently contains over 750 volumes—a Very Short Introduction to everything from Psychology and Philosophy of Science to American History and Relativity—and continues to grow in every subject area.

Very Short Introductions available now:

Available soon:

For more information visit our website

www.oup.com/vsi/

Patricia Daley and Ian Klinke

HUMAN GEOGRAPHY

A Very Short Introduction

OXFORD
UNIVERSITY PRESS

OXFORD
UNIVERSITY PRESS

Great Clarendon Street, Oxford, OX2 6DP,
United Kingdom

Oxford University Press is a department of the University of Oxford.
It furthers the University's objective of excellence in research, scholarship,
and education by publishing worldwide. Oxford is a registered trade mark of
Oxford University Press in the UK and in certain other countries

© Patricia Daley and Ian Klinke 2025

The moral rights of the authors have been asserted.

Published in the United States of America by Oxford University Press
198 Madison Avenue, New York, NY 10016, United States of America

British Library Cataloguing in Publication Data
Data available

Library of Congress Control Number: 2024952136

ISBN 9780192869302

Printed and bound by
CPI Group (UK) Ltd, Croydon, CR0 4YY

MIX
Paper | Supporting
responsible forestry
FSC® C013604

The manufacturer's authorised representative in the EU for product safety is Oxford University
Press España S.A. of El Parque Empresarial San Fernando de Henares,
Avenida de Castilla, 2 – 28830 Madrid (www.oup.es/en or product.safety@oup.com).
OUP España S.A. also acts as importer into Spain of products made by the manufacturer.

Contents

Acknowledgements

We are very grateful to Hashem Abushama, Maan Barua, Linda McDowell, Gillian Rose, Rory Rowan, and Thomas Turnbull for comments on individual chapter drafts and, in some cases, the initial book proposal. Three anonymous referees did much to improve the project, as did Thomas Bartles-Smith, who helped us collect media coverage on human geography as a field. We are extremely thankful to Latha Menon for her patience and help in making this book come together. Ian made his final touches to the manuscript while a British Academy Mid-Career Fellow and a visitor at the Danish Institute of International Studies. Patricia is grateful to Jesus College Oxford for providing research support.

List of illustrations

Human Geography

Chapter 1
What is human geography?

A few years ago, the British Broadcasting Corporation (BBC) produced a documentary about the Himalayas. It features the British comedian Michael Palin, known to many viewers as part of the Monty Python collective. Palin seems to be having a good time. He meets people, visits temples, and tastes dishes. In one episode he attends the border crossing ceremony between India and Pakistan at Wagah, which remains to this day an elaborate spectacle, featuring impressive uniforms, spectator stands, raised legs, and displays of disapproval between the two rivals' border guards. But although there is hostility, Palin is keen to emphasize that the two sides are ultimately cooperating. They lower flags and close the gates together. In Wagah, it takes two to tango.

Palin's tone in describing the two rival states' military choreography is jolly. Clearly, the British comedian who will a few years later head the Royal Geographical Society is poking fun at a region in which borders still matter. It is 2004. In Europe, borders are still being pulled down. The European Union's enlargement is making it easier for Eastern Europeans to work and live in the West. The 2016 Brexit referendum is political light years away. But somehow, the documentary insinuates, the inhabitants of India and Pakistan are still caught up in the past.

1. Border closing ceremony at Wagah, 2016.

The India–Pakistan border is a useful device to illustrate how human geography speaks to the bigger issues of our time. The border ceremony reveals the futility of nationalism and national borders. The similarity of the two uniforms (Figure 1) and the cheering crowds on both sides seem to imply that these are people obsessing about minor differences. A discussion of the military drill at Wagah can also help to demonstrate the point that borders require human bodies to *perform* them. Don't we too perform when we take off our glasses and show our passport to border security?

Geopolitically, both states have been allies of the United States, but this has not meant that they have got along. In the past, there have been military standoffs and outright war. Visible from outer space since India installed floodlighting a few years ago (Figure 2), the 2,000-mile India–Pakistan border is one of the most militarized frontiers on earth. Further conflict seems likely. It is worth noting that both states are nuclear powers. While India tested its first nuclear weapon in 1974, Pakistan followed suit in 1998. Climate

2

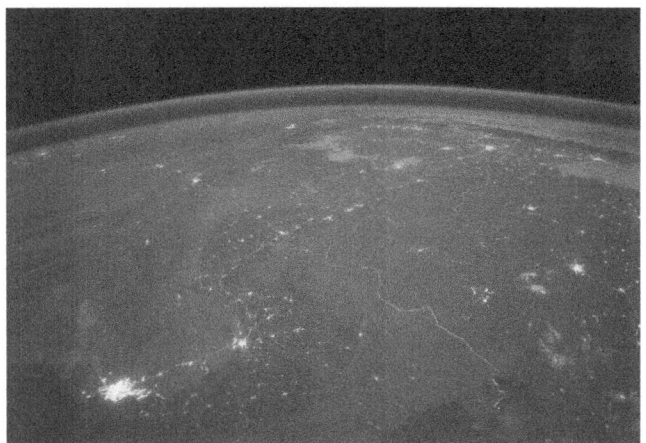

2. India–Pakistan border at night, as viewed from International Space Station, 2015.

scientists have modelled that a regionally contained nuclear war between India and Pakistan could not just lead to the devastation of the two countries, but could also prompt a global 'nuclear winter', featuring a temporary cooling of the planet, crop failure, and mass starvation.

The border at Wagah has a colonial origin. It was the British 1947 partition of India that resulted in its creation. The so-called Radcliffe line sought to divide India crudely into Hindu-majority India and Muslim-majority Pakistan, the latter initially including what is now Bangladesh. It was named after Cyril Radcliffe, a British official who was tasked with finding a territorial solution. He had never visited India. His 'solution' prompted forced migration and mass murder. Precise numbers are hard to come by, but over 10 million are said to have fled their homes, while over a million may have died in the violence that followed. Although it differs from the other mid-20th-century British colonial crimes such as the Bengal famine or the crushing of the Mau Mau uprising in Kenya, partition is often listed amongst the empire's worst atrocities.

As you will have guessed, we are already doing human geography. Human geography can seem broad, so broad that few things lie outside its purview. And yet, there is a direction. More often than not, human geographers grapple with the big problems of our time: economic inequality, wars, forced migration, racial injustice, gender inequality, and the climate crisis. Human geographers are not alone in tackling these issues. But they tend to distinguish themselves from others by employing a spatial lens, by posing the question of *why what is where, and how it came to be there*. To answer this question requires a curiosity about the things around us and a skilled look for what is interesting about them.

Contemporary human geography has come a long way from the subject's 19th-century imperial origins and its tendency to use the environment (geology and climate) to explain regional and social differences. Instead, geography has embraced approaches that allow more nuanced explanations to understand human relationships with space and place. This shift has not just been driven by the limitations of past explanations. Change has crucially also come from more diversity amongst researchers and educators. Working-class, women, non-European, Black, Indigenous, and queer geographers have enriched the tapestry of geographical approaches and concepts tremendously in recent decades.

Before progressing any further, it is helpful to understand human geography's position within the larger academic discipline of geography. Geographers tend to fall into two main divisions: physical geographers who examine earth system processes from the perspective of the natural sciences and human geographers who study the human aspect of geography from a social sciences perspective. Human geography thus seeks to examine the bigger picture and integrate forms of knowledge that are elsewhere treated as separate enterprises: history and economics, for instance, or politics and environmental science. Like its physical counterpart, human geography thus offers a holistic and synthetic approach.

Human geography can be further broken down into a number of *sub-disciplines*. Perhaps the most important are economic, historical, political, social, and cultural geography. These sub-disciplines have their own journals and academic cultures. They speak to one another and build bridges to neighbouring fields such as economics, history, politics, sociology, and anthropology. More recently, a distinctive field of environmental geography has formed which seeks to bring human geography once again into a closer dialogue with the natural sciences. Beyond these six, there are further *issue-based sub-fields* such as urban, development, transport, or digital geography which cut across these six sub-fields.

Another way to divide the field up would be to recall that human geographers are almost always experts on a particular world region, a specific country, or smaller cultural unit. Some of us are Latin Americanists, others have expertise on China, others again on particular minority groups. This usually entails acquiring an in-depth understanding of a given society or social group, its culture and language. Although some geographers find the study of areas limiting, usually because their object of interest elides regional or national boundaries, regions remain a crucial organizing principle.

In some quarters of the field, researchers define themselves first and foremost as theorists. Arguably, we all theorize—even those of us who have never picked up a book about geography. But it is true that different approaches—Marxist, critical, feminist, more-than-human, or decolonial geography (which will be introduced as we progress through the chapters)—are sometimes used to break up the field into rival camps. Some of these theoretical approaches are sizeable enough to have their own journals and canonical texts. But more often than not, human geographers congregate around key concepts such as space, place, scale, power, environment, and embodiment. This is perhaps a more inclusive way of conceiving of what human geography is and

5

does—because it allows others to join in. Let us begin by tackling the two most foundational of these concepts: space and power. Modern human geography is unthinkable without this couplet.

Thinking about space and power

We negotiate space in our daily lives without giving it much thought. Think about your local village, town, or city, your workplace, school, hospital, church, mosque, mandir, eruv, and even your home. How often have you asked yourself who made this space and for what purpose? How is it disciplining you into particular kinds of behaviours? What could you simply not do here? How might others experience this space, and what might explain those divergent experiences? What, in other words, are the fundamental power relations that define this space?

The more we think about it, the more difficult it becomes to ignore the fact that our lives are constituted through space. They have a *here* and a *there*. Both territory and private property, two of the most important modern institutions, function by enclosing space. Others increase our mobility and connectivity by opening space up. What is the modern world, if not the channelling of human bodies through particular spaces: the hospital, the classroom, the shopping mall, the motorway, the open-plan office, the concentration camp? Of course, no classroom or camp are ever the same, but they repeat certain functions which can be deduced from the rules and behaviours that govern them.

How are these rules and behaviours mediated? They are encased by infrastructure, by technology and architecture, by concrete, steel, oil, and semi-conductors. But they are also quite clearly shaped by imagined geographies, by ideology, religion, and other belief systems that organize space for us. These are *constructions* in the sense that they depend on processes of building and assembly. They are *social*, that is, neither natural nor timeless. This means that they can be disassembled, too. Underneath and within these constructions is *power*.

This may sound a little abstract. Power is hard to perceive and grasp. But while it is in a sense invisible, it produces tangible effects. Think about the following: what would it mean for you to have a voice in a beauty parlour, or a prison for that matter? The authority with which you could speak in each of these settings would depend on whether you were there as a customer, an employee or the owner, a guard or a prisoner. It would be contingent on the intersectional constitution of your identity in terms of class, race, gender, and so on. Your voice, in other words, would be amplified or silenced by historically thickened power structures that constitute both the beauty parlour and prison and your position within it.

It would seem then that we cannot really think about space outside of power. But what then is this thing we call power? We can define it in many ways. Power is essentially domination, and it therefore has violent dimensions. The threat and exertion of violence compels others to do things they do not want to do. And yet, violence is often the tool of the weak. It relies on weapons to compensate for a lack of legitimacy. Power also has an economic dimension. Here, Marxist geography offers an important lead. If you want to understand urban transformations such as ghettoization or gentrification, you have to grapple with the ways in which private property, capital, and social class produce space. Finally, we can add that language itself exerts power over us. It matters how space is represented and constructed in language. The institution of the prison is not just bricks and mortar, iron and razor wire. It is a symptom of how our society thinks and speaks about crime. This is something that geographers have been keen to point out since the 1980s.

So far, we have presented space as a matrix in ways that might make it seem a little finished, overpowering, and unbreakable.

We are in danger, as Nigel Thrift reminds us, of treating things and human beings as mere 'flies trapped in a web of coordinates'. Indeed, we have to be careful not to work with a notion of space (or time for that matter) in which power structures overdetermine meaning and which fails to explain *why things would ever change*. Not all spaces are fixed. The prison system has transformed since the Middle Ages, whether for better or worse. Even bounded space (think of a territory like that of India or Pakistan) relies on an *elsewhere*, on relations of things, treaties, and performances that are beyond that bounded space.

People are not just connected to the places in which they currently find themselves. Diasporic communities still identify, in complex ways, with their erstwhile homeland. Some spaces may even lack a dominant architectural form. The virtual space of the 'market' comes to mind or technological interfaces like the smart phone and its never-ending stream of content. Digital space or cyberspace provides new, almost instant access to communities across the globe. Only a few decades ago, building communities online would have been very difficult and would have taken significant time. The political consequences of this new connectivity are profound, and they are still playing out around us.

Such seismic changes highlight that space is hardly fixed for very long. The rules that govern space are routinely broken, architecture can be put to new uses, and technology can fail. A beauty parlour can be turned into a bakery and a prison's security system can break down. Power relations are never complete, they tend to fray around the edges. (How would things change otherwise?) And to the degree that space and power are inseparably intertwined, this means that space too is potentially fragile. The geographer Doreen Massey captures this well when she argues that because space is a process (it needs to be made and remade) it is never a closed system and thus open to different kinds of futures. However much it is laden with power, it is still characterized by 'loose ends and missing links'.

This does not mean that topography is unimportant or feeble. The production chain of the smart phone is localizable, as are the satellites and mobile phone masts needed to transmit content via our devices. Markets too need to have a here and a there, often enabled by governments, to unleash their force. Yes, we can do things with space, though, more often than not, space does things with us. It circulates and fuses; it permits and enables; it restricts and forbids. To grapple more fully with this force that is space, human geographers have cultivated the skill of seeing global patterns in local things and, conversely, spotting the local exception that subverts the global pattern. And it is not just the local and the global that we can use. There are a whole range of geographic scales at which we can trace processes: the home, the neighbourhood, the city, the region, and so on. The power relation between these levels of analysis shapes fundamentally the ways in which social issues play out.

A very important scale, and one which is at the core of feminist enquiry, is the human body. It is near impossible to imagine our experience of space outside of our embodied experience. How would we make sense of a forest at night without our senses? Think of the sound of cracking underwood, the moonlight on the path ahead, or the pain we feel when we stumble and fall. And how would we think without a gut feeling? Bodies, moreover, are different and sense differently, as geographers of disability have reminded us. Human geography can thus never entirely be a quest for universals, for things that are true everywhere and always. It is a form of enquiry that is bodily and historically interested. In order to understand how things change, we need to know where they came from.

How we got here

Now that we have established a basic sense of space and power as core concerns for contemporary human geography, it is instructive to trace how our discipline got to where it is. The earliest history of geography is very significantly entangled with that of cartography. Humans have made maps for thousands of years for economic, military, legal, and spiritual reasons. It is helpful to know where a river flows, where fertile land lies, who inhabits it, and what divine authority has been derived from it. And yet, the practice of mapping is not timeless. For reasons we will explore later in this book, there was an explosion of cartographic activity that coincided with the birth of the modern territorial state and the advent of European colonialism. This cartographic eruption is key to an understanding of what it means to do geography in the present.

Histories of the field tend to emphasize geography's Greek and Roman, and to a lesser extent Arab, origins. But it is crucial to understand that the academic discipline of geography emerges only truly in the first half of the 19th century, with the dreamy polymath and explorer Alexander von Humboldt and the dry armchair academic Carl Ritter. Although very different sorts of intellectuals, they both established geography as a holistic science: you had to appreciate the wholeness of our planet to understand its particularities. When they both died in 1859, geography was on an upward trajectory, not least because it was taking shape outside of the academy. Geographical institutions like the aforementioned Royal Geographical Society, founded in 1830, intertwined science and colonialism. This was the allure of geography: it could serve as a practical form of science which collected useful knowledge for the colonial state, naming, categorizing, and ranking. Boosted by an age of European imperialism, geography grew. By 1885, there were 12 professorial chairs in geography in Germany, then the academic centre of gravity in Europe. Many of these posts were held by human geographers, all of whom were men. The anglophone world moved more slowly, but here too key departments were founded in Oxford, Cambridge, Chicago, and Berkeley at the turn of the last century.

Somewhat ironically, early human geography offered an attempt to integrate the social and natural sciences at a time when academic knowledge was becoming ever more specialized. If you wanted to understand a nation's economy, human geographers argued, you had to understand its geology. The discipline was initially defined by an attempt to understand how nature influenced and indeed 'controlled' human societies. Early 20th-century geographers like the American Ellen Churchill Semple even went so far as to explain the emergence of slavery in North America and the American Civil War by reference to climate and topography. We know this line of reasoning today as environmental determinism, an approach which fell out of fashion in the 20th century with a realization of the complexity of social worlds. Today there are virtually no academic geographers who write from an environmentally determinist perspective. And yet, it lives on for instance in the popular books of Tim Marshall, whose best-selling *Prisoners of Geography* spells it out: geography controls and determines.

This then was the deeper meaning of colonial geography. For if geography is destiny, then domination by the 'haves' over the 'have nots', of civilizations located in a temperate climate over those in the tropics is simply *natural*. This strand of thought did much damage during the 20th century. When Nazis promised to secure new 'living space' in Eastern Europe (Germany had given up on Africa after losing its colonies in the First World War), they did so to a significant extent because they had encountered the ideas of Ellen Semple's professor, the geographer Friedrich Ratzel. Ratzel argued that peoples and states struggled for space in much the same way as plants and animals did in the natural world. He had written of a 'battle of annihilation' between European settlers and the Indigenous Americans. The outcome of this clash, he believed, was inevitable—for the Indigenous had a 'weak grip on the soil'.

But not all geographers were of Ratzel's ilk, not even in the 19th century. Take the vision promoted by the geographer and theorist of 'mutual aid' Peter Kropotkin. The Russian anarchist famously outlined the task of geography as one of countering the forces of nationalism, colonialism, and racism. Like others, Kropotkin thought that geography was an ideal school subject and hoped that it might teach children that political borders were mere relics of humanity's barbarous history and thus best overcome.

By the early 20th century, geographers decided that it was their job to make sense of regions, believing that this task was to geography what the study of time was to historians. This was in some ways a return to Humboldt and Ritter. But it turned out to be an overly descriptive exercise. By the 1960s, geographers had already become bored with it. Instead, they became enthralled by the language of mathematics, by quantitative methods and grand abstractions. The new approach was known as spatial science—and it did not remain unchallenged for long. So-called humanistic geographers began in the 1970s to re-centre human experience in geographical enquiry. Scholars like Yi-Fu Tuan questioned the scientific pretence behind spatial science, instead diverting attention to the realm of human experience: how is it that we become emotionally attached to particular places? To answer this question necessitated a return to realms that had largely been rendered *ungeographical* after Humboldt: art, philosophy, and aesthetics. It also opened human geographers up to new and more poetic ways of writing. These were important advances which continue to reverberate through the field today. They broadened the scope of what might count as legitimate research in human geography. And yet, spatial science has lived on, boosted in the 2000s by the arrival of big data and geographical information systems (GIS).

Ultimately, regional geography, spatial science, and even humanistic geography all ignored political questions. Such apolitical forms of enquiry proved a dead end to many geographers. What subsequent decades have seen is thus precisely a fundamental repoliticization, first in the form of Marxist, then feminist, and finally in decolonial human geography. Today there is a plurality: Black geographies, queer geographies, work on disability, etc. They explicitly set out to produce situated knowledge. These approaches ask the fundamental question: who are we and how does our identity affect the research we do and the ideas that we promote?

Similar lines of enquiry are taken up by decolonial geographers. Inspired mainly by Latin American and Indigenous scholars in the global North, decolonial geography challenges the universalization of European knowledge systems. It starts by asking questions, such as why and how European science, as an approach to understanding natural and social phenomena, became universal. What other forms of knowledge were elided and silenced in the process? Decolonial scholars trace a direct link between the universalization of European knowledge systems and the expansion of European colonialism, and the political power associated with it. They argue that epistemic violence—the act of suppressing non-European knowledges—provides the basis for other forms of indirect and direct violence. Decoloniality is a movement to bring about global change which reveals forms and practices of resistance by colonized and formerly colonized peoples. It calls for the legitimizing and valuing of non-European knowledge systems, thus enabling the recognition of a plurality of ways of knowing, of which the European is just one. For Indigenous scholars, decoloniality envisions a society that embodies a restorative and transformative form of justice and the principle of mutual coexistence. Kropotkin, without doubt, would concur.

This book

Human geography provides answers to some of the most important challenges of our time. If we wish to understand contemporary political struggles over economic inequality, forced migration, racial injustice, gender inequality, global warming, or indeed the reverberations of colonial border drawing, we must grasp the ways in which these are fought *over* and *through* space, both physical and abstract. We must, in other words, come to terms with the imagined, embodied, and often violent cartographies of a wide range of spaces that define our world and the social relations and political struggles that unfold around them. It is in contemporary human geography that we can find clues about the ways in which space and power have been constructed, subverted, and resisted over time.

This book recognizes what the geographer Neil Smith describes as the complicity of geography with empire but draws on progressive advances to introduce its readers to new trends in 21st-century human geography. Students and general readers will discover in this book a guide to the most important approaches, debates, and authors in human geography. They will also find a vital assessment of how spatial power formations continue to structure society, with or without our consent.

Rather than a comprehensive but necessarily superficial whistle-stop tour of human geography, this *Very Short Introduction* offers a taster of the field. It does so in the form of six journeys—or cuts—into the subject matter. We ground our discussion in spaces and concrete places. We have selected six spatial formations which have been pivotal to recent geographical debate and which are also defining features of modern life. They are the colony, the pipeline, the high-rise, the border, the workplace, and the conservation area. The afterword takes us to outer space. We use these as entry points into a wider survey of the discipline. We hope that what human geography is and does will become clear as you progress through the book. But we also recognize that there are many aspects of our field which we will have to leave untouched. This book is thus very much meant as a starting point.

Chapter 2
The colony

In June 2020, a statue of a long-dead Englishman was toppled, defaced, and thrown into the waters of Bristol harbour (Figure 3). His name was Edward Colston, and he was known, if known at all, for his philanthropy. Roads, schools, and other public buildings all bore his name, celebrating his contributions to the city of Bristol. Only very few Bristolians knew how Colston had amassed his wealth.

There was something spontaneous about the disposal of this symbol. The statue was pulled down during the Black Lives Matter protests that had erupted following the murder by a police officer of the African American George Floyd in Minnesota, USA. But the anger that motivated the protesters in Bristol had been brewing for many years. The ripples formed as the bronze statue hit the water soon spread far beyond the harbour.

Who was this man whose name featured so prominently across the city, people began to ask. Edward Colston was a slave trader. From 1680 to 1692, Colston was a senior executive and deputy governor of the Royal African Company, the corporation that dominated the Transatlantic slave trade during the 17th and 18th centuries. He played a key role in the enslavement of over 84,000 Africans, of whom over 19,000 died on their journey across the Atlantic. As the mercantile activities through which Colston

3. Colston statue being pulled down, Bristol, 2020.

obtained his wealth came under the spotlight, many could see for the first time the socio-spatial connections between the individual, his beneficiaries, the port of Bristol, the British state, its colonies, and empire writ large.

The toppling of the statue became in many ways a teaching moment on the politics of public space. Even two centuries after the 1833 Slavery Abolition Act, it revealed that Britain was still commemorating slavers. Political geographers have raised questions about the power dynamics underlying memorialization by showing how the presence of statues in public spaces is used to perpetuate a particular version of the past by those with power and how this, in turn, affects people's experiences in such spaces. Consequently, such research has led to debates on how this process might be democratized.

Prior struggles over Colston's legacy had led to very little tangible change. And there was certainly more than history at stake. With descendants of enslaved peoples amongst the protesters, the event made clear that we all still inhabit the aftermath of slavery, a colonial present if you like. In the early 2020s, Black Britons in England and Wales are more than three times as likely to live in social housing than their white counterparts. They are four times as likely to be murdered, as data from the Office of National Statistics reveal.

When the transatlantic slave trade emerged in the 16th century, it transformed the economic geography of the modern world. The exploitation of enslaved peoples took place in the colony—a geographic space characterized by specific forms of political domination, resource extraction, and social relations of production. We tend to think of colonies of European countries as far away places, located in the global South, but this discounts former colonies such as Ireland and Greenland, as well as Russia's colonies, all of which are in the global North. Colonies come in different shapes and forms, the most important of which are trading outposts, mining colonies, and settler colonies. Colonies create around them a violent geography which, as Achille Mbembe writes, divides the world into two legal spaces: one where European law is applied and the other where this juridical order can be suspended. Throughout history, colonies have been frontier-like spaces in which various forms of violence could be experimented with, and where pacification tended 'to assume the face of endless war'.

The geography of empire

We often hear people speak of colonies and the process of decolonization as things that occurred in the past. The United Nations Special Committee on Decolonization, first established in 1961, reports that more than 80 former colonies have gained independence since 1945. A mere 17 non-self-governing territories remain in 2023. Small independence movements still exist in some of these territories, although the call for political decolonization or self-rule is still resisted by remaining colonial powers. Some territories, such as Martinique and Guadeloupe, are treated officially as external departments of France. Though not insignificant, fewer than 2 million today live under direct colonial rule, a figure dwarfed by those who no longer do, some 750 million people.

But focusing on formal decolonization can blind us to the persistence of colonialism, for even colonies which have gained political independence suffer under the continued dominance of Euro-American states and corporations. Former colonized states are locked into relationships that perpetuate their subjugation and dependency. The term neocolonialism is often used to explain the persistence of colonial relationships which might involve indirect political or economic control. This has spurred on 21st-century movements for decolonization. These movements demand a move beyond 'paper independence' to address the hegemony of European knowledge systems, political structures, racial hierarchies, and science, and the consequential devaluation of Indigenous thought and cultures.

At its core, colonialism is a system of domination of one people over another which has political (such as territorial control), economic (extraction of labour and resources), and cultural dimensions (imposition of value systems). To facilitate this extractive process, new governance structures are introduced even where state organization existed previously. Colonialism often introduces a new language, education systems, gendered hierarchies, the codification of Indigenous traditions into customary law, and the production of new landscapes reflecting colonial land management practices and cultures.

Infrastructure, particularly roads and railways, is typically built to facilitate extraction—the legacies of which remain prominent in many countries in the global South. To this day, such infrastructural projects are used to exemplify an ideology of modernization. It is through the idea that a colonial centre helps its (former) colonies to catch up, to *become modern*, that colonialism reproduces itself. In some countries, surviving colonial infrastructure has also acted to constrain efforts to reorientate economies and regional integration.

As well as generating wealth for corporations, investors, and aristocrats, colonies served as destinations for Europe's surplus populations, places where states disposed of their unwanted orphans, and criminal elements with the establishment of penal colonies (e.g. Tasmania and the Seychelles). Some 68 million Europeans migrated to the colonies in North and South Americas, Australasia, and Africa. Most of them came from Germany, Ireland, Britain, Italy, Spain, Portugal, France, the Netherlands, Norway, Sweden, Poland, Russia, and Ukraine.

Settler colonialism constitutes the establishment of permanent and initially agricultural settlements, a process which goes hand in hand with the violent replacement of Indigenous populations. Settler colonies are usually supported by a metropolitan centre. Even where such colonies develop some degree of self-government, they usually institute a political and social system that replicates that of the metropole while continuing their dominance over the Indigenous peoples where the latter have not already been exterminated. Settler colonialism usually describes the former colonies of Canada, USA, Australia, New Zealand, and South Africa, Zimbabwe, and Namibia under apartheid. But it can also be found in the West Bank of Palestine.

Other forms of colonialism tended to occur in places where European settler populations were relatively small in comparison to Indigenous communities. Initially, chartered companies were given rights to explore, colonize, and extract the resources from territories claimed by European states and monarchies. In addition to Colston's Royal African Company, Cecil Rhodes's British South Africa Company, the German East Africa Company, and the Royal Niger Company (now Unilever) were amongst those operating in Africa, often with considerable independence. The East India Company (1660–1874) ultimately began to resemble a state, a polity with its own police, ports, etc. and traded in a wide range of commodities, such as tea, guns, and textiles. The profitability of trading in these new consumer goods led to the creation of new global trading networks that marked the first phase of globalization.

European companies faced competition from rivals as well as local resistance. Profits were greater if they had exclusive control of particular territories. Companies overthrew, tricked, enticed, or forced local rulers to sign treatises giving them exclusive access to the resources in these lands. Companies such as the East India Company had their own police force, militias, and currencies. But it was the intensity of the competition between European capitalists and the need for military and regulatory protection that led some companies to lobby their home states to establish colonies—that is, to take direct political control, often expanding geographically from coastal trading posts. Colonial domination was often carried out by force. Although wars against rebellious peoples were euphemistically termed 'pacification', such military expeditions often involved scorched earth policies—the destruction of communities, massacres, forced displacement, and the use of concentration camps. Such violence could acquire genocidal dimensions, as the 20th century's first genocide in German South West Africa shows. The list of colonial genocides is long and covers all continents.

Extraction of wealth was the primary purpose of the 15th century's voyages of discovery that were sanctioned by the Catholic Popes in a number of so-called papal bulls. These edicts provided divine justification to European dispossession and capture of the land of Indigenous peoples and their conversion to Christianity. Europeans had knowledge of the wealth in the Eastern hemisphere due to the long-established trade routes used by Arab traders and the 12th-century Italian merchant Marco Polo. Gold from

Africa had already been in circulation in medieval Europe. Technological developments in shipping and navigation enabled the seafaring nations of Europe to circumnavigate the globe faster and drove an insatiable appetite for riches and knowledge.

The science of taxonomy expanded through the widespread use of Carl Linnaeus' classification system that renamed every known species in the world. In the name of science, animals were captured, killed, pickled, stuffed, bagged, and taken back to Europe. Even the human remains of Indigenous peoples were stolen for 'scientific study' or for public display in museums and human zoos. It is only in the 21st century that colonized peoples' demands for the return of human remains have been acknowledged, leading to a small number of cases to repatriation.

Geography as a field of knowledge played a crucial part in exploration and colonization. Founded in 1830 and still active today, London's Royal Geographical Society (RGS) has provided a crucial meeting place for adventurers, scientists, and merchants. The RGS was, and in many ways remains, a place to learn about the world beyond Europe. The explorations it funded were never just driven by the discovery of places unknown to Europeans, but also by the quest for precious metals and stones, such as gold, silver, and diamonds, and later new agricultural commodities, such as sugar, tea, coffee, silk, and cotton textiles, bringing new sources of wealth to the imperial centre that would fuel the industrial revolution.

If you wanted to be a geographer, you had to put your boots on and board a ship. Halford Mackinder, the first person to hold an academic post in geography in Britain and the founder of the geography department of Oxford University, was a bookish sort of man. To establish his credentials amongst the community of geographers, he felt compelled to climb Mount Kenya in 1889. Exploration provided a way of heightening white Victorian men's masculinity as daring and adventurous, as conquerors of nature. In recent decades, post-colonial geographers have revisited this period of exploration. Using archival research, they have looked not just at the field's key figures, but also at the hidden histories visible only in the margins of the archive. These reveal the existence of female explorers such as Mary Kingsley, who rarely recounted their experiences directly due to gender norms in Victorian and Edwardian England. Similarly, we knew next to nothing about the Indian explorer Pundit Nain Singh and others who guided European men to places that they 'discovered'. Research on Mackinder has also uncovered the acts of violence he sanctioned, including taking an expedition through a famine-stricken land, and his involvement in the murder of eight of his African porters.

For Mackinder, who continues to find admirers on the political right today, the role of geography was to aid the exercise of power by providing both cartographic and mental mapping of the world and by instilling an imperial mindset in every British child. But there was a wider culture in which the description and mapping of overseas terrain were packaged for a wider public. The more exaggerated the accounts of rivers, mountains, deserts, and peoples, the more they aroused public curiosity. To gain fame and resources to pursue further adventures, explorers collected and brought back biological specimens and accounts of physical features that were mapped and often given European names. This was the context in which the geographical discipline operated. It is no surprise, then, that some topographical features were named after presidents of the RGS, such as the Aberdare Mountains in Kenya or the Murchison Falls in Uganda.

The violence of imaginative geographies

To gain and retain support in the metropolitan centres, European colonialism relied on 'imaginative geographies' about the non-European world. The Palestinian-American intellectual Edward Said used this term to describe the linguistic production (in the widest possible sense) of an exotic and mythical space, 'the Orient', which stretched from Turkey to China. His basic idea was that it mattered how *other* places were imagined, not least because of what this said about how the West thought about *itself*. It was by characterizing 'the Orient' as variously backward, traditional, irrational, and uncivilized that the Occident could emerge as advanced, modern, rational, and civilized. The colonizing 'West', in other words, needed—and still needs—the colonized 'East' as its counter-image.

Geographers have extended Said's initial formulation of Orientalism to think about the ways in which the Soviet Union was framed during the period known as the Cold War. Although initially focused on how the Orient had been represented in literature, art, and academic knowledge, Said's formulation of Orientalism had always been highly political. The point was that the violence perpetrated by European colonial powers had a cultural underbelly which in the early 2000s became particularly visible in the ways the Western powers legitimized a new round of military aggression in the Middle East. This serves as a reminder of the violence inherent in the imaginative geographies Said first systematically uncovered. Territorial conquest, expropriation, dispossession, displacement, extermination, torture, and even forms of sexual violence were all justified by Europeans' belief in their racial, technological, and cultural superiority.

The 'Orient' was not the only imaginative geography through which European colonialism operated. Influenced by the work of Edward Said, post-colonial geographers have revisited the literature and representations of places and inhabitants produced during the colonial period and their enduring legacies. The vast continent of Africa, with its diverse peoples, cultures, and physical environments, is often falsely represented as a single country and as synonymous with barbarism and poverty. The persistence of these representations allows for simplistic interventions by other countries in African affairs and for Africa's wealth to be extracted and looted. Even today Africa is known in some corners as the 'Dark Continent', a vast space in need of enlightenment, including by Christian missionaries. Lucy Jarosz contends that the persistence of the metaphor of the Dark Continent flattens places and people and obscures the political, economic, and cultural forces of colonialism as they have unfolded in Africa. Europe's epistemic dominance relied on such enduring stereotypes. They serve the colonial present.

European colonizers sought to refashion the world with Europe as its role model. The Egyptian political scientist Samir Amin uses the term Eurocentrism to describe the often-implicit idea that Europe is the most advanced of human societies with the most desirable social order. The philosophical transformation that had taken place in Europe during the period of the Enlightenment meant that rationality and objectivity and the rule of science and technology were considered the hallmarks of a modern society. The colonized were expected to mimic Europe's modernity, as it arrived first with its transport systems, modernist architecture, and consumer culture.

Language mattered here, too. Colonizers attempted to reorganize the social worlds of colonized peoples, classifying them into 'tribes' or ethnic groups, and spatially demarcating their homelands or ethnic territories. In some countries, such as Nigeria, large geographical expanses of people with different linguistic dialects were merged into one ethnic group, for example, the Yoruba-, Igbo-, and Hausa-speaking peoples. In other countries, such as Tanzania, almost each dialect was classified as belonging to a distinct ethnic group. Tanzania was left with an estimated 125 'tribes'. In countries such as Rwanda and Burundi colonial administrators turned social classes or castes into distinct 'tribes' with fixed and exclusionary identity boundaries. People were expected to remain in their clearly demarcated ethnic territories. Movement between these was only encouraged for those recruited to work on colonial projects. In those cases, workers were given passes that restricted them to an employer for a clearly defined period. Concurrently, new linguistic maps emerged as English, French, Spanish, and Portuguese were enforced as dominant languages.

Racial ideology adds a pivotal layer. The idea that one group of people is superior to others in all or most respects—physically, cognitively, and culturally—enabled the mistreatment of those who were considered at the bottom of the evolutionary ladder (Figure 4). Racialization, the process by which people with different phenotypes are placed in a hierarchical order, was evident in Europe from the 15th century. Religion and modern science came together in a perverse way. The papal bulls that allowed the colonization of the Americas justified the capture of land because Indigenous peoples were considered heathens and

4. European man in a sedan at Bombay (now Mumbai), British India, before 1860.

in need of conversion to Christianity. Nineteenth-century race scientists, on the other hand, used Charles Darwin's theory of evolution to give scientific rationale to their construction of a hierarchy of human beings. Some of Darwin's expeditions were funded by the RGS.

The physical characteristics of the colonized were measured against those of the (white) European male, who was considered the most highly evolved of human species. Sylvia Wynter describes how European migration to the Americas and their encounter with Indigenous peoples led to Europeans assuming the universal figure of Man, who was defined by his humanness and contrasted with Indigenous peoples who were denied their humanity and naturalized—essentially treated as wild, akin to fauna. Such racial thinking validated the extreme violence executed against Indigenous peoples. In geographical thought, the aforementioned environmental determinism linked racial and cultural differences to people inhabiting specific environments and climatic zones. Environmental determinism was particularly popular in North American geography in the first half of the 20th century.

In addition, racial differences were used to explain the technological superiority of Europeans over the peoples they encountered. Racial thinking justified the capture and utilization of resources, especially the expropriation of land. This allowed for the claiming of Indigenous lands as supposedly unoccupied, barren, and unused. Such land could then be 'discovered' and owned by Europeans. A quasi-legal principle that allowed for the capture was that of *terra nullius*—a term derived from the Latin meaning 'nobody's land'. The concept was widely used across the colonial world to justify land appropriation and written into law in Australia. In Indigenous cultures, land had been communally accessed. The concept of private property had to be introduced to allow Europeans to have inalienable (legal) tenure.

Colonialism and development

A crucial sphere in which colonialism has persisted is in development. The latter's emergence as a policy goal and wider political agenda is often traced to the inaugural speech of US President Harry Truman in 1948, where he entreated former European colonies to allow the West through the United Nations to assist them in achieving economic and social progress. Modelled on the Euro-American experience, development was promoted to newly independent states in the post-1945 era of formal political decolonization. Post-colonial states adopted Western political structures and institutions, often from their departing colonial powers. However, geographers have challenged the myth of the 'European Miracle', as arising from some special kind of 'Europeanness', and instead seen it as rooted in the immense wealth generated by colonialism itself.

Theories that became known as development or modernization approaches emerged after the Second World War to explain how countries could progress in a linear fashion. But often there was an even cruder agenda at work. A good example of this is the American economist and erstwhile US national security adviser W. W. Rostow's 'Stages of Economic Growth' model. Published in 1960, Rostow's model became a blueprint to assess what stage a country was at in its development trajectory. The book's sub-heading 'A non-Communist manifesto' revealed it as an attempt to deter former colonies from turning to communism as a route to modernization.

Both capitalist and communist development required fundamental transformations in all aspects of economic, cultural, and social life. Cultural 'backwardness' was often given as a reason for the economic and social conditions in formerly colonized countries. Post-colonial states were placed on a linear scale from underdeveloped to developed. As colonies became independent, they were subjected to guidance by development experts from Western countries, including from former colonial powers, and international aid organizations which had ostensibly arisen to provide charitable assistance to poor people in the global South.

New imaginative geographies emerged. One example was the construction of 'the West and the rest', whereby a developed West was positioned as the opposite of an underdeveloped external world. There was a racial component to this. While 'the West' was occupied predominantly by people racialized as white, 'the rest' was inhabited by those racialized as Black, Brown, and Yellow. These geopolitical divisions were filled with social characteristics that were represented as natural. For example, endemic poverty was attributed to natural (e.g. climate) and cultural (backward traditions) factors. Western dominance in the global institutions (The United Nations, World Bank, International Monetary Fund) established after the Second World War meant that the West became the model to follow and the primary site for modern ideas and practices.

Western modernity, in seeking to erase all other ways of knowing, has been used as a basis for continued intervention by imperial powers in their former colonial territories—manifested in development and humanitarian aid and through support for political regimes that ensure the continuation of the extractive processes. Economic development that involved industrialization and the transformation of raw materials into consumer goods, despite being the basis for capitalist development in the global North, was rarely encouraged in post-colonial states, and this neglect was justified by the arrival of neoliberalism in the 1980s. Neoliberal theory, which began in the University of Chicago, promotes the free market, a minimal state, and individualism and allows for state withdrawal from development and social welfare activities. Countries that have been subjected to neoliberal austerity measures, in the form of Structural Adjustment Programmes imposed by the World Bank and International Monetary Fund as part of their debt management strategies, were advised to focus on their comparative advantage of exporting raw materials for production or consumption elsewhere. These resources include bauxite, copper, and high-valued agricultural commodities with seasonal demands in the global North. Despite Western support, large swathes of the populations in global South countries are impoverished, and their development trajectory has shown slow progress. Since the 1960s, development geographers have exposed the failure of development policies and practices to transform people's lives for the better and have argued that 'development' has functioned as an ideology promoted by former colonial powers. Jim Blaut attributes this failure to the diffusion of ideas that promote Europe's trajectory as the model for change, while failing to note that progress in Europe depended on the extraction of resources from elsewhere. Extending this critique, Amber Murrey and Patricia Daley call for the abolition of international development as it disempowers locals through its perpetuation of colonial/racial ideas, practices, and policies.

In the 21st century, some global South countries such as Singapore, China, and Malaysia have seen levels of economic growth surpassing those in the global North. China, following its own model of modernity, has promoted infrastructural development as the primary engine of economic transformation to other global South countries. The persistence of neocolonial relationships between former colonial powers and their ex-colonies and the use by Western countries of colonial imaginaries to pursue their military and development agenda in global South countries has led geographers to rethink their frames. Divisions of the globe into 'First' and 'Third World' (the 'Second World' being that of the former Communist bloc) and 'developed' and 'developing world' struggle to capture what is going on today. Even though the global North/global South divide, which we have already employed in this book, also can be interpreted as a form of binary thinking, the fact that the term 'South' was used amongst former colonies seeking to reimagine their world makes this division momentarily acceptable as a tool of decolonial thought and political praxis.

Decoloniality manifests differently in formerly colonial places across the globe. For North American geographers, decolonial means an outright refusal to accept white supremacy, anti-Blackness, and settler colonialism as given, especially the violence that each of these produces. In settler colonial territories, the demand is for land and the recognition of Indigenous ontologies or ways of being in the world, especially Indigenous understandings of the relationship between humans and the non-human world as counter to violent and environmentally damaging resource extraction. Globally, decolonial means transcending the dominance of European thought, or its universalism, by promoting non-European ways of being in the world. It seeks to 'provincialize Europe' and enable pluriversal (multiple) ways of being and knowing. Decoloniality requires the dismantling of racial hierarchies and their resultant dehumanization of non-European peoples. Amongst Black diaspora communities in the UK city of Bristol, it is about reckoning with the injustices of the colonial past and forging more inclusive, non-racial societies in the present.

Chapter 3
The pipeline

Most readers will know the scent of fuel. You only have to walk past a petrol station to get a whiff. Its distinctive smell is in large part caused by benzene, a compound which improves fuel efficiency and engine performance, and which lends it a sweet note. Some people are drawn to it. It may be the memory of childhood road trips. More likely, it is the substance's ability to induce euphoria, relaxation, and numbness when it enters the bloodstream via the nose or mouth. Indeed, petrol sniffing is known as a low-cost form of substance abuse amongst poorer populations throughout the world. It can lead to the irreparable damage of one's mental and physical health.

Crude oil, also known as petroleum, is all around us. It is pumped out of the ground, shipped across the globe, and fought over by corporations and states. Oil-derived fuel powers cars, tractors, aeroplanes, and tanks. It is used to make plastics, textiles, and sports equipment. The liquid is so mobile and versatile that it is used across the spectrum of production. All of this happens because there is an enormous gap between the energy it takes to extract and consume a barrel of oil and the energy that can be derived from it. And conveniently, once it is burned, it is no longer your responsibility. Or so we believed.

There is a darker side to this flammable chemical substance. Entire states can become dependent on its export in ways that cripple their economies and feed corruption. We speak of 'petrostates'. In 2010, the Deepwater Horizon oil spill released 40,000 barrels into the ocean—per day—damaging ecosystems and coastal communities. Although the biggest accidental oil spill, it was only one of many. More menacing are the consequences for global warming. When oil is burned, it releases high amounts of carbon dioxide, a greenhouse gas, which powers climate change by trapping heat in the atmosphere. Today, oil has become a symbol of a specifically 20th-century way of running the global economy: boom and bust, exploit and deplete, extract and pollute.

What might a human geography of oil look like? In 1915, the US geographer John Rich wrote an essay entitled 'Notes on the Human Geography of an Oil Field'. Rich wanted to explain the social impacts of oil drilling in Illinois and elsewhere in North America. He noted that the discovery of oil brought with it an impressive infrastructure of derricks, pumping houses, storage tanks, and pipelines. And unlike in the case of coal, iron, or zinc, the exploitation of oil did not require a large labour force once a field had been established. Rich then proceeded to describe the psychological effects that accompanied the discovery and exploitation of oil reserves, particularly the quickly spreading 'rush' whenever a new source was found. 'Excitement is in the air, everyone is talking oil, and every stranger is suspected of being an oil man seeking leases,' he observed. These sensations, he argued, were all prompted by oil's material properties. It was, or so he claimed, the fact that oil lies beneath the earth's surface and with very few above-ground indications of its presence that introduces an element of uncertainty, mystery, and risk, a 'gambling element'.

What Rich was missing of course was a sense of a more complex economy surrounding the extraction, commodification, and consumption of this non-renewable source of energy. What made people who sought those leases so exhilarated, if not the desire to earn copious amounts of money with their share of the black gold? Rich was neither the first nor the last to frame fossil fuels as a vast sphere of riches that was merely waiting to be exploited. Such framings and arguments about their causal power have remained popular. They are present when we speak of entire regions as no more than a storehouse of fuel or when we invoke oil as a prime mover of political decision-making without considering the wider context within which oil matters.

What have human geographers done to correct and complicate accounts that construct such a direct and causal influence of geography on the human psyche and politics? Firstly, they have examined the flows of capital in relation to the movement of oil and how both of those sustain the global economy. Secondly, they have accounted for the ways in which oil is extracted and turned into fuel. This necessitates a focus on the labour employed in the process and the conditions under which this labour is given. Thirdly, geographers have addressed the political struggles that surround the drilling and transport of oil. In doing so, they have paid crucial attention to the locations in which violent dispossession and accumulation quite literally *takes place*.

The pipeline is a networked political space, a space where things flow. There are other spatial devices needed to extract, transport, and commodify fossil fuels: the oil rig, the pumpjack, the tanker, the refinery, the petrol station, and so on. But the pipeline is crucial because of its vulnerability, which has made it such a highly politicized form of infrastructure. While other things can be moved through pipelines (e.g. water, natural gas, and sewage), we focus on the black liquid that stands so directly for the self-destructive moment at which humanity stands today.

Energy transitions

Although oil is often viewed as inorganic, it is in fact formed from organic matter. Crude oil is made of algae, microorganisms, and marine organisms that have been 'slow cooked' for millions of years under pressure and heat, usually a few miles under the earth's surface. Oil has thus been sitting in underground reservoirs for a very long time before humans decided to drill, process, transport, and burn it to convert its energy into mobility and affluence.

Against the geologic timescales, the dawn of the fossil fuel age came very recently, in early 19th-century Britain, and it was coal rather than oil that first put the industrial revolution on steroids. While coal had mainly been used as a way of heating homes, energy had otherwise been drawn from renewable sources, chiefly wind and water, as well as human and non-human bodies and the burning of wood. The rise of steam engine technology in the 18th century, however, was a game-changer. Indeed, by the 1830s the steam engine had replaced the waterwheel as the dominant source of energy in this important sector. Whereas watermills were susceptible to droughts and flooding, coal was more resilient. It could easily be delivered and stored in places where it would be needed and moved via railway. Most importantly, while watermills had to be built along rivers, steam engines could be installed in cities, where labour was abundant. Ultimately, the transition happened due to the profits that could be made from this new source of energy.

Fossil fuels, in other words, must be understood from their outset as existing in a 'social relation'. They emerge in a certain context, an industrializing capitalist society, and immediately shape that society, too. What matters ultimately is how these fuels are embedded in the relation between capital and labour. As Andreas Malm reminds us,

> [N]o piece of coal or drop of oil has yet turned itself into fuel. No humans have yet engaged in systematic large-scale extraction of either to satisfy subsistence needs. Rather, fossil fuels necessitate commodity production and waged or forced labour as components of their very existence.

In many ways, industrialists found in fossil fuels and the machinery they power a compensation for what they saw as the shortcomings of human labour. Compared to human bodies, coal and oil do not just release more energy; they have also proved more obedient and reliable sources of energy. This profit motive behind the extraction of fossil fuels remains in place to this day. Global coal use may have peaked, but companies and investors are still making money with it. The global economy must phase out coal rapidly if it wants to hit the targets of the 2015 Paris Agreements, a key international treaty to tackle climate change. But in the wake of Moscow's 2022 invasion of Ukraine and the sanctions on Russian energy, profits in the global coal industry tripled.

The second crucial energy transition took place in the first half of the 20th century. Like coal, petroleum had mainly been used in a domestic context, as lamp oil. But it was not until the rise of the automotive industry that this surplus was fully realized. Oil's higher energy density, when converted into petrol and jet fuel, allowed for the powering of smaller vehicles, including those that can fly. But it also led to active efforts to remove alternative modes of transport. If you look at a map of the Berlin tram system, you will see that even today it only extends to the former Eastern part. In the capitalist West Berlin, tramways were dismantled in the mid-20th century. The car was hailed as *the* future mode of transport.

Almost immediately, the rise of oil changed the geopolitical calculations that states made (Figure 5). Already before the First World War, Britain began switching its navy from coal to oil, greatly improving the speed of its ships. Because it needs particular geological conditions to form, oil is very unevenly distributed across the globe, prompting states that are not well endowed with petroleum to seek the control of oil-producing states and regions. One of the reasons why Nazi Germany's invasion of the Soviet Union was unsuccessful was the Germans' failure to capture the

5. Huntington Beach oil field, California (c.1930s).

oilfields of the Caucasus in 1942, thus constraining their army's mobility and effectiveness. Oil has remained crucially important in international affairs ever since.

Despite the enormous forces which coal had unleashed, it had its downsides, particularly once industrialized economies had become dependent on it. In its heyday, coal passed through few hands and along fixed routes where it could be slowed down, disrupted, or cut off entirely. And this, of course, is precisely what coal miners learned to do to great effect. In the late 19th- and early 20th-century North America, they were three times as likely to go on strike than their peers in other industries. Strikes which began in coal mining often spread into neighbouring industries like railways and shipping. These strikes were not always successful, but they were a menace to mine and factory owners and could occasionally destabilize governments, too. Indeed, one of the reasons the British navy switched to oil was because it allowed it to evade the problem of its strike-prone Welsh coal miners.

By the mid-20th century, a transition to an oil economy had removed this 'problem' (which was of course in reality a response to inequity). This was because oil did not, as John Rich had noted in 1915, require a large labour force. And those workers who were employed by the oil industry could be scrutinized *above* rather than left to their own devices *below ground*. There were other advantages. Oil companies were no longer reliant on fixed railway lines which could be blocked. More easily than with coal, they could ship their product in large quantities across oceans using tankers, if necessary, avoiding politically unstable regions. And in large quantities it was certainly moved. By the year 1970, oil constituted more than half of global seaborne cargo. It was shipped by companies which did not have to abide by the kind of labour laws which coal miners and others had fought hard for over the preceding century.

Given oil's prevalence across the production chain, the price of oil remains perhaps the single most important price in the global economy. By the 1970s, it was states, not workers, that had begun to disrupt the flow of oil for political reasons, immediately causing prices to shoot up. Recession followed. When the Islamic Revolution in oil-rich Iran threatened to weaken America's grip on the global oil market even further, Washington decided to police oil itself. As US President Jimmy Carter famously declared in January 1980, '[a]n attempt by any outside force to gain control of the Persian Gulf region will be regarded as an assault on the vital interests of the United States of America, and such an assault will be repelled by any means necessary, including military force'. In the years following the announcement of the 'Carter doctrine', the United States established a large permanent troop presence in the Middle East and surrounding areas and has since used these forces to intervene militarily on a number of occasions to enforce what it perceives to be its national interest. Although we can argue with the interpretation that it was 'all about oil', petroleum undoubtedly played a role in the USA's decision to invade Iraq in 2003.

Trouble in the pipeline

Coal, we have already established, was more profitable than renewable resources, but the accumulation of capital from coal was threatened by industrial action. This has not been the case with oil. And yet, oil too has its pressure points. Oil and gas require a sophisticated array of technologies on their journey to be turned into carbon: pumps, valves, delivery trucks, and so on. One place that has remained particularly vulnerable is the pipeline. This is because pipelines are expensive, because they often cut through politically significant land, and because they are usually quite long. The latter fact makes it difficult to secure them comprehensively. Often, those who steal from a pipeline or sabotage it can get away before they are caught.

Today, there are over 2 million miles of pipelines spread across the globe (which dwarfs e.g. the length of the world's railway network). These pipelines carry natural gas, biofuels, and of course oil. The oil, usually alongside other substances such as natural gas, is pumped out of the ground and sent to a refinery. This is where the pipeline provides a mode of transport which is cheaper than any other land-based method, though exact costs will vary depending on terrain. We tend to imagine and map pipelines in horizontal ways, as a grid, network, or tree. In reality, of course, these steel tubes need to be understood in their verticality: they are mainly buried underground where they are safer from human interference, but often at the mercy of earthly forces, such as water, landslides, and earthquakes. The liquid nature of oil and the pressure under which it exists in its untapped state too lend it a certain unruliness that the pipeline seeks to contain and channel. Pumps are inserted into the pipeline to keep the pressure up and the liquid moving. Pipelines need to be reliable and robust, not least politically, for petroleum attracts conflict and violence.

While oil's uneven distribution across the globe has prompted geopolitical conflict and war, its transportation networks are often subject to struggles over land rights and locally specific environmental regulations. Pipelines, especially new ones, are crucial symbols of a society that is struggling to decarbonize. And occasionally, things do go wrong. There are leaks and accidental explosions which can cause significant destruction. But perhaps more crucial are the political struggles surrounding key pipelines.

Readers will have heard of Nord Stream, two controversial offshore pipelines built to carry Russian natural gas to Germany under the Baltic Sea, which were blown up in September 2022, probably by Ukraine. Nord Stream was contentious not just because of the environmental damage that the natural gas would do when burned. It was a geopolitical liability. Its existence allowed the Russian state-owned energy company Gazprom to deliver cheap gas to Western Europe, bypassing states such as Poland and Ukraine that were directly feeling the impact of Russia's imperial aggression. It was felt that the pipelines made it less likely for the recipients of Russian energy, chiefly Germany, to support Kyiv's armed struggle against Russia. Nord Stream certainly made Russia less dependent on existing pipelines in Ukraine. Once Nord Stream was no longer feasible, Germany had to move fast to become independent from Russian oil and gas. It did so in a number of ways, one of which was to increase its consumption of coal, that dirtiest of fossil fuels.

What might happen when we take less the larger geopolitical conflict as a starting point for our understanding of pipeline politics, but rather the opposition surrounding particular pipelines? Here, the environmentalist struggle against two key North American pipelines serves as an instructive case study. Completed in 2017, the Dakota Access Pipeline transports crude oil from North Dakota to a refinery near

6. Pipes for Keystone pipeline, 2009.

Chicago. Keystone XL was planned to carry highly polluting tar sands from Canada to the Gulf of Mexico, but was ultimately scrapped in 2021 after years of popular opposition (Figures 6 and 7). What was particular to these campaigns was their populist dimension, meaning that there were attempts to forge a popular movement around a clear friend/enemy distinction. Despite the 'people versus pipelines' framing employed by many activists, there was in fact a complex political landscape surrounding these pipelines. Changing alliances between environmentalists, Indigenous groups, and ranchers formed in the effort against the oil majors—but rarely shared the same objectives. Although the conflict played out on land which had been appropriated from Indigenous Americans in the 19th century and which remained contested, radical critiques of settler colonialism were often muted so as to not break up the coalition. Thereby a politics of the lowest common denominator was often the modus operandi.

7. Protesters, San Francisco, 2017.

Valuable lessons can be learned from less well-known pipelines, too. The BP-led Baku–Tbilisi–Ceyhan pipeline was commissioned in 2006 to deliver crude oil from the Caspian Sea to the Eastern Mediterranean. Russia saw the pipeline as a challenge to its dominance in the energy market, not least because it bypassed its ally Armenia. There are other and more local tales to be told about the politics of this pipeline, stories about enchanted trees, the vicissitudes of 'corporate social responsibility', the suspension of local labour laws, and the way in which information (economic, managerial, but also scientific) can drown out politics. This case reveals how the political can nonetheless find articulation in some quite mundane material questions, for instance about pipeline-coating agents that crack and fail. While some villagers along the pipeline claimed to have had walnut trees in their gardens in order to be compensated by the oil company, others moved their beehives closer to the pipeline for the same reason (bees produce less honey when there is noise pollution and vibration from construction sites). Hidden

41

behind the grand question of oil geopolitics, in other words, are other forms of politics, struggles which are shaped by the availability of information.

Africa too has seen its fair share of oil geopolitics. Despite fast growth, the continent's GDP is still exceeded by the revenues of the 10 largest oil companies. When it was constructed in 2000, the 660-mile Chad–Cameroon oil pipeline was the largest private onshore investment on the continent, necessitating vast land appropriation (an area as large as Benelux) and affecting over 1,000 villages. But as in the case of the Baku–Tbilisi–Ceyhan pipeline, here too a locally specific but no less telling set of political relations comes into vision. For, as Amber Murrey shows, the consortium's attempts to make the pipeline disappear from public view and the corruption surrounding the infrastructural project attracted existing local witchcraft knowledges. Petroleum itself was rendered supernatural, less for its ability to generate wealth than as a way of making sense of the arcane networks of power that surrounded the creation of this wealth. There was little in the way of organized resistance, but the language of *la sorcellerie* (witchcraft) was nonetheless highly political, drawn upon even by those who did not believe in it to expose the ruthless exploitation which hydrocarbon extraction brought with it along the pipeline.

Pipelines are a reminder that fossil fuel capitalism has a geography. It exists in particular locations. The idea of oil as part of a global and networked flow of goods and our way of mapping it horizontally can blind us to this reality. But it is crucial to appreciate this geography because it reveals the pressure points and weak spots of such extractive economies and the myriad political struggles that surround them.

What to do?

Global warming was clearly an unintended by-product of the fossil fuel era. And yet, knowledge of fossil fuels' driving role in climate change was long suppressed. Oil companies paid lawyers and PR firms, scientists, journalists, and politicians to sow seeds of doubt about anthropogenic climate change, despite the fact that the industry had evidence from at least the late 1950s, as Ben Franta shows, that its products would likely cause sea-level and global temperature rise by the end of the 20th century. The oil industry's efforts evolved over time. Initially, it had questioned whether global warming was happening at all. Later, it tried to discredit the science that showed it was the burning of fossil fuels that was causing the problem. When even that no longer seemed to convince, the fossil fuel industry began investing heavily in greenwashing campaigns, designed to make them look as though the oil majors were now the agents of decarbonization. Despite their efforts at convincing us that they have reformed their ways, these companies are continuing what they do best: extracting petroleum and reaping profits.

It is important to understand that there was never any inevitability to a world forged by pumpjacks, pipelines, and petrol pumps. Even today, it is worth distinguishing between those parts of our economy that are dependent on oil and those that could be disentangled from fossil fuels. There remains a window of opportunity for decarbonization. But it is highly unlikely that oil companies themselves will be the agents of this transition; they simply have no incentive in abandoning existing reserves. Nor should we necessarily expect the change to come from politicians and political parties. Recent years have seen a strong alliance emerge between the fossil fuel industry and far right political formations which have sought to mobilize car owners. It is no coincidence that today's climate deniers tend to have their base on the right.

One timely question is whether there are other ways to enforce the decarbonization of our economies. Fossil fuel divestment campaigns sprang up on university campuses in the 2010s, demanding that their institutions rid themselves of investment into oil and gas. Drawing on earlier divestment campaigns concerning arms, tobacco, and slavery, they highlighted the immorality of profiting from assets that would ultimately harm future generations. But they also made economic arguments: were fossil fuels not likely to end up as stranded assets and thus unlikely to yield much in the long term? Although success has thus far been localized, there is momentum as younger and environmentally active generations of students are coming through the ranks. One of the key achievements of fossil fuel divestment campaigns has thus been a politicization of fossil fuels.

Most contemporary climate action movements, including Extinction Rebellion, have restricted themselves either to non-violent protest or to obstruction (of motorways or airports). When the activists Ruby Montoya and Jessica Reznicek vandalized the Dakota Access pipeline in the hope of preventing it from being built, they faced charges including high fines and up to 110 years in prison. Few of us would question that the suffragettes had the right to strike against property when they demanded the vote for women. The struggle against apartheid in South Africa too made use of sabotage. And nobody would criticize those who brought the Berlin Wall down for using brute force. But while there is consensus when we look at past wrongs that violence against slavery or the holocaust was legitimate, violence against the fossil fuel industry has not (yet) been granted the same status, as Andreas Malm notes. Despite the efforts of environmentalists, pipelines are not exclusively, perhaps not even primarily, regarded as forms of political infrastructure. They are seen as property.

Human geographers will continue to ponder where a world of pipelines, oil spills, and global warming has left us. In her 2018 book *A Billion Black Anthropocenes or None*, Kathryn Yusoff sets out to rethink humanity's relationship to the geological formations that came to matter in the age of fossil fuel capitalism. There has been a move, thus far unsuccessful, to name a geologic epoch after humans, the Anthropocene (*anthropos* is Greek for human), in all likelihood humanity's last. Human activity has left an impact not just on the planet's climate and ecosystems, but will leave one in the geological record, too. Yusoff notes these debates, but emphasizes that the forces which have been unleashed through the burning of fossil fuels have not been produced evenly by humanity, but by a much smaller part of humanity, those at the forefront of colonial and capitalist expansion.

Yusoff turns our attention to how geology is itself intertwined with white supremacy. She is not just interested, more obviously, in how geology was constituted as a Eurocentric form of science, but also how humanity's journey deeper and deeper into the earth in its quest for natural resources has tended to expose the bodies of the colonized to harm. It was enslaved Africans that were brought to mines of South America by European colonizers. Black and Brown bodies were exploited by mining companies as something of a shield, an extra layer, Yusoff argues, to protect white colonial lifestyles powered by the sale of these resources from the latter's toxic characteristics. Yusoff thus plays with the double meaning of stratification as both a geologic (the earth as layered) and racial structure (the hierarchies established and exploited by European colonialism).

Such forms of environmental racism persist in 21st-century extractive zones. In the global South, the extraction of oil is promoted by international development agencies, such as the World Bank, as a critical development strategy, bringing untold wealth—oil equals money. Instead, what happens, in what Michael Watts terms these 'oil frontiers', is that oil companies unite with government officials and security forces to ensure that the bulk of the profits are offshored, while local inhabitants suffer from oil pollution and poverty, including fuel shortages. In 2011, the UN estimated that it will take 30 years at a cost of $1 billion dollars to clean up the Niger Delta in Nigeria, where oil spills, flares, and acid rain have contaminated land and water, destroying the livelihoods of local people over a period of 60 years of oil extraction.

Quitting oil

As humans adapt to a hotter planet and consider more radical options for political change, they are also pondering their own place within the current historical moment. Filling up a car at a petrol station is no longer a politically innocent act (if it ever was), but one which is entangled with ethical questions about the conditions under which this liquid was produced and transported and about the damage it will do, including to those not yet born.

At some point in the mid-20th century, oil became a 'lifeblood', as one clichéd expression has it. By the 1970s, oil was so important to the global economy and the modern way of life that it had to be secured militarily by the United States. Despite a recent turn to renewable energy in the early 21st century, the global economy remains heavily dependent on the burning of fossil fuels. In 2019, and thus on the eve of the Covid-19 pandemic, around 80 per cent of the world's primary energy was generated by burning oil, gas, and coal, dwarfing wind and solar energy. Given that the Carter doctrine, which remains in place to this day, ensures access to Gulf oil, it is perhaps no surprise that the US military has an enormous carbon footprint. If it were a country, it was reported in 2019, it would be the 47th largest emitter of CO_2—at similar levels to countries like Peru or Portugal.

As the drilling and fracking of oil continues, the pipeline remains a key symbol of a fossil fuelled capitalism. It also reminds us that despite all the talk about the death of location in an age of globalization, the oil economy remains rooted in concrete locations—which are now increasingly targeted by environmentalists. The steady rise of environmental consciousness has not prevented the vision of a nation powered by fossil fuels from remaining surprisingly resilient.

Chapter 4
The high-rise

On 14 June 2017, a refrigerator caught fire in a kitchen in Grenfell Tower, a social housing apartment block in West London. The fire spread rapidly throughout the building due to the combustible exterior cladding that had been installed only recently as part of an £8.6 million refurbishment. An estimated 72 people died in what was the worst residential fire in the United Kingdom since the aerial bombing of the Second World War. Most of the tenants living in Grenfell Tower were from low-income ethnic minority households. Some of them were refugees.

Located in Kensington and Chelsea, the wealthiest borough in London, Grenfell was surrounded by some of the most expensive residential homes in London, home to British celebrities and Russian oligarchs alike. Even though the borough council was comparatively wealthy, it had opted for a cheap and flammable form of rainscreen cladding, in part to beautify the building. Architects, local government officials, construction companies, building product manufacturers, fire safety testers, and services were all in some way implicated in the Grenfell tragedy. But while the disaster was the outcome of a coalescence of factors, urban geographers have shown how the UK government's programme of economic austerity from 2010 onwards and the diffusion of responsibility associated with the free market had created its conditions. Less government intervention led to the loosening of building standard regulations, including a reduction in the number of building inspectors.

In the years that followed the fire, the surviving tenants' struggles to be rehoused and to receive compensation illustrated the limited pool of affordable housing in London and the failure of accountability when multiple stakeholders might be at fault. Grenfell also shows the extreme social inequalities that are prevalent in most cities, and how, in the global North, they can intersect with racial difference and citizenship status. It became clear too that it was not just the high-rise blocks of the poor that were affected. Leaseholders in new apartment blocks across the country were also vulnerable because similar cladding had been used. The Grenfell Tower fire was a spectacular event, partly because of its shocking visual imagery (Figure 8) that was shared almost instantly on social media and the challenges faced by its residents in escaping from the building. But it was also an

8. Grenfell fire, 17 June 2017, London.

iconic representation of the failure of vertical architecture as a way of organizing urban life.

High-rise buildings are difficult to construct and can be inconvenient as well as dangerous to live in. But they are also the cheaper option in places where land is expensive. While the growth of high-rises in late 19th-century New York was certainly enabled by the availability of more sturdy materials and the invention of the elevator, they were driven first and foremost by high land prices and ground rent, coupled with increased demand for offices, housing, and industries. For property developers, it was more profitable to build upwards, and, if they owned the freehold to the land, they could maximize ground rent from leaseholders. It is therefore no coincidence that vertical forms of living are bound up with the capitalist economy. Indeed, the super-rich of Kensington and Chelsea are likely to build extra storeys under their period mansions.

Vertical construction is not an entirely recent phenomenon. High-rises in the global South pre-date those in the global North. Those in the Yemeni town of Shibam, located in the Ramlat al-Sab'atayn desert, are mud-brick high-rises dating back to the 16th century. Rising to some 11 storeys, they were designed to protect their inhabitants from war and flooding and were common for Yemeni cities. But the ascent of financial capital since the mid-1970s led to an urban boom around the world, most evident in China, India, Mexico, South Korea, and Chile. In 2024, more than half of the world's population lived in about 10,000 cities, of which 22 were considered megacities having over 10 million inhabitants—think of Chongqing (32m), Lagos (16.4m), Delhi (16.7m), and Tokyo (13.2m). Indeed, cities with the fastest growth rates are in China, Nigeria, and India. High-rise buildings are portrayed in such cities as symbols of economic development and modernity, whether in financial districts or residential complexes. Today, the skylines of Hong Kong and Shanghai, Kuala Lumpur, Gurgaon, Seoul, or Tokyo are not dissimilar to those of London, Los Angeles, or New York—some are even grander. Skyscrapers are indicative of economic power. This might explain the long-running competition to build the tallest building in the world, which, in 2024, is Dubai's Burj Khalifa, standing at 828 metres.

What drives contemporary high-rises in the global South is the concentration of capital and rapid urbanization. China has surpassed the USA with the highest number of tall buildings, with the majority built after 2020. Height competition and 'excessive' and risky overbuilding occurs as the space and scale of construction does not match the economic strength of the cities. In China's rapid urbanization, the high-rise has become the typical mode of housing for the country's high-density urban population, including its middle classes. But Chinese villagers too are being forced into concentrated high-rises, losing their access and entitlements to farmland.

In the global North, high-rises, such as Grenfell, were once seen as the solution to the problem of 'slum' housing. Notable examples are the *Habitations à loyer modéré* (HLM) or modern rental housing on the outskirts of Paris. These social housing high-rises were built in the *banlieues* (suburbs around 15 miles from the centre of Paris) to house the white urban poor and immigrants from North Africa and former French colonies. The *Banlieues* have suffered from years of neglect, lack of access to services, high rates of unemployment and crime, and heavy policing. Such conditions have prejudiced French public opinion against those living in the *Banlieues*, who are then subjected to stigmatization. In the USA, a comparable project was that of the Pruitt-Igoe complex in St Louis, Missouri. Built in 1954 to replace overcrowded tenements, Pruitt-Igoe comprised 33 11-storey blocks designed to house 10,000 people. However, by the 1970s, Pruitt-Igoe, inhabited mainly by African Americans and neglected by the state, had become so squalid and crime ridden that it was demolished. At the time the destruction of Pruitt-Igoe was said to symbolize the unviability of the high-rise as a decent living space for families in the city. In the UK, there is a law that states that children should not be housed above the seventh floor, but they were in Grenfell—and 18 of them died on 14 June.

Cash and the city

Cities have their origins as trading centres, industrial locations, and sites of government—military, democratic, and religious. Catalhöyük, in the Anatolia region of Turkey, was the site of the earliest known city, dating from about 7400 BCE to 5200 BCE. It was in many ways a proto-city in that it lacked streets. Houses had to be accessed by walking from roof to roof. Other ancient cities have been found in modern-day Egypt, Mexico, China, West Africa, and the Amazon region of Ecuador. The term city is derived from the Latin word *civitas* or citizenship, while urban refers to life in a city. Historically, the urban population has increased due to natural growth within cities, as well as rural–urban migration, often caused by wars, forced displacement of peasant farmers, and endemic poverty. Rural depopulation and migration to industrial towns and cities in England was quickened by the 1773 Enclosure Act, which allowed landlords to fence off common land used by landless peasants. Similar practices of land dispossession have occurred in global South countries. In India, Brazil, and Indonesia, land appropriation for large-scale plantation agriculture and mines, mechanization, coupled with low wages for rural labourers, and low prices for small farmers' crops, contribute to the unsustainability of rural life.

Under capitalism, cities have become sites in which surplus capital is absorbed into and disinvested from property and infrastructural projects. Cities thus become defined by the concentration, flow, instability, and unevenness of capitalist development. In London and Birmingham, pockets of deprivation have grown in neoliberal Britain at the same time as areas of wealth concentration and overconsumption. Capital investments in cities have varied across time and space from the construction of factories, tenement dwellings, and shopping malls to the residential and office building blocks of urban renewal and gentrification projects. Since land values and rents in cities are often the highest in any country, urban property markets tend to be the most competitive.

The drive to turn housing into a lucrative economic asset has meant that late 20th- and early 21st-century urban renewal projects have tended to reduce the amount of housing available to low-income citizens, thus increasing competition in the housing rental market and limiting the housing stock available to newcomers to the city and to growing families. A further negative effect of this financialization of housing could be seen in the US subprime mortgage crisis which triggered the 2007–8 global financial crisis. It occurred when low-income households that were enticed by property developers and banks to take out mortgages due to cheap credit found they were unable to service their loans because of interest rate hikes. Mortgage lenders, who had promoted homeownership, rushed to evict owners when loans became unsustainable. Over 3.8 million foreclosures occurred between 2007 and 2010. When the housing bubble burst, banks began to go bust, leading to significant state intervention.

Subjected to neoliberal free-market principles, urban housing policies have involved privatization of social housing and restriction on its construction. In cities such as London and Amsterdam, social housing has been sold to individual tenants, charities, and other non-governmental organizations (NGOs), as well as private equity companies. In some cases, these new landlords have deliberately embarked on gentrification. Gentrification is a process by which low-income households are displaced from deprived areas of the city and replaced by high-income middle-class ones, often accompanied by infrastructural improvements. Gentrification of working-class and largely immigrant areas of Inner London started in the 1970s.

It was spearheaded by artists and creatives, who were swiftly followed by young professionals seeking larger and cheaper working and living spaces respectively. At this stage, the original inhabitants could no longer afford to live in these areas. In East London, gentrification was accelerated by the redevelopment of the London Docklands area known as Canary Wharf and the Lea Valley area by the 2012 Olympic games. The Notting Hill area around Grenfell Tower, famous for its Caribbean carnival, had undergone a similar process of gentrification in the decades before the fire. Indeed, in 2017 the Grenfell tower block was one of the final areas of social housing in the neighbourhood.

Although it began in North American and European cities, gentrification has spread globally. And yet, gentrification in cities in the global South is largely state led, as part of urban redevelopment and beautification projects, often designed to attract investment. Property developers working with city authorities can bulldoze shacks in informal settlements, or displace street market traders, in projects to aggressively 'clean up' or 'modernize' urban sites. In the Brazilian cities of Salvador, São Paulo, and Rio de Janeiro, such gentrification projects involve the displacement of low-income Black and Indigenous people from their neighbourhoods and their replacement by white newcomers, a strategy not uncommon in formerly colonized cities, with euphemistic language used to hide racial and financial intent.

On a smaller scale, individual house owners are also enticed to generate extra income from the short-term home-sharing rental market. As with the Uber car-sharing services discussed later in this book, Airbnb is a global digital home-sharing online platform matching homeowners to short-term rental demands, almost mirroring the services provided by hotels. The popularity of Airbnb has led to accusations that it has contributed to displacement of permanent residents, due to the shortage of available and affordable long-term housing for rent and higher housing prices in cities that were already under housing pressures. Anti-Airbnb protests have sprung up in North American cities, such as San Francisco; and since 2020, protesters in 22 European cities have demanded changes in European Union legislation to allow public authorities to monitor Airbnb platforms. In February 2024, the EU introduced new registration rules to increase transparency in the short-term letting sector, aimed at targeting illegal activities without affecting tourism-dependent regional economies.

Authorities in some cities have sought to counter the marketization and financialization of housing through rent control. Started in England in 1915 (though discontinued in 1988), regulations on capping the maximum rent landlords can charge their tenants have enabled affordable housing for private renters in cities such as New York, Copenhagen, and Geneva. Rent control laws have also covered security of tenure and building maintenance. But under neoliberalism, the erosion or removal of rent controls has led to rent increases and no-fault evictions. Having faced exorbitant rent hikes over a 20-year period, renters in Berlin campaigned and won a 2021 referendum on the issue: 59.1 per cent of those who voted were in favour of expropriating properties owned by large corporate landlords. With politicians reluctant to act, an independent expert commission ruled in June 2023 that expropriation was legal.

Rent hikes and precarious employment have contributed to the rise of homelessness in cities. While New York had 62,000 registered as homeless in 2022, Los Angeles had 65,000. These tended to be single-household adults. In contrast, in 2018, the 3 million homeless in Manila, the capital city of the Philippines, mainly consisted of family groups. Despite the United Nations principle on the right to shelter for all, neoliberal states have no obligations to provide housing for their economically marginal citizens. Alex Vasudevan documents the urban squatting and social movements campaigning for affordable housing in cities as far apart as Vancouver and Frankfurt, including the 'Reclaim the city' movement in Cape Town, South Africa, consisting of tenants and workers. In Europe and North America, a wave of 21st-century anti-squatting legislation has criminalized the act of making a home in an empty property. Vasudevan's discussion of these protest movements draws on the sociologist Henri Lefebvre's concept of 'the right to the city' as an improved right to urban life, where 'informal' or 'illegal' occupation of premises demonstrates the urgency of the need for social justice in housing and signifies how alternative forms of shared living can occur in cities. Lefebvre saw 'the right to the city' as extending beyond the right to access housing or urban amenities; it should involve active participation in urban design, as well as rights against police abuse and unfair property laws—in effect the right to be self-governing.

Segregation

Evidently, urban landscapes are marked by social differences and hierarchies. Urban geographers have long mapped and sought explanations for the level of class, racial, gender, and religious segregation in cities. Money, infrastructure, and politics affect how people move and where they live. A combination of actors—city councils, urban planners, property developers, banks, mortgage lenders, insurance companies, landlords, homeowners, tenants, and the police—all contribute in some way and to varying degrees to the spatial formation and fortification of urban inequality.

Perhaps the crassest form of social inequality is racial segregation. Segregation was most pronounced in North American and South African cities, where discrimination and legislation resulted in neighbourhoods that were predominantly white, Black, Latino, and Asian. In apartheid South Africa (1948–94), people categorized as Black and Coloured were placed in designated townships away from the white community—the most famous of which was Soweto, near Johannesburg. These segregated communities experienced differences in the quality of life and

9. Segregational signs at a South African train station, before 1972.

access to services, which, despite legislation outlawing discrimination, have been stubbornly persistent (Figure 9).

Some cities are divided because of the allegiance to a particular state or nation, as the example of Belfast shows. The history of the Northern Ireland conflict is rooted in the colonization of Ireland by settlers from Britain in the 17th century. Today, it takes on the form of a clash between Irish Republicans and Unionists, where the former tend to be Catholic and the latter Protestant. At the heart of the conflict, which is marked by decades of armed resistance, police violence, terror against civilians, and military intervention, is the question of whether Northern Ireland should belong to Ireland or the United Kingdom. Even decades after the 1998 peace agreement, which brought power sharing to the region, paramilitary organizations continue to operate in Northern Ireland. In Belfast, murals and flags, particularly in working-class neighbourhoods, are still used to show allegiance to one of the two communities. Some neighbourhoods are separated by high barriers and there are frequent clashes with the police. Ninety per cent of schooling remains segregated and marriages across the divide are still surprisingly rare.

As in other divided cities, such as Mostar, Nicosia, or Jerusalem, division is not simply an act of political identification. It is about public space and access to infrastructure, such as transport, health care, and housing. The question of who controls the police is of course crucial, too. Such struggles are difficult to resolve and in most divided cities violence remains a possibility, even where it has become less frequent.

Despite their high visibility, cities divided along political lines are in fact unusual. It is more common for cities to be divided economically. In a sense, all cities where housing is unequally distributed have a tendency towards segregation. Gated communities and ghettos are the most obvious manifestations of such economic segregation, but it is present too in the most mundane of questions, such as whether you can afford to live in a certain part of town or visit a certain restaurant. We often think of global South cities as prime examples of extreme forms of social inequality. Our gaze turns to informal settlements in Jakarta or Rio de Janeiro as evidence of the wretchedness of city life, where high unemployment and state neglect leave the majority of city residents eking out a living in overcrowded and insanitary spaces. But the processes driving inequality in London or Los Angeles are clearly iterations of the same dynamic we can observe in Jakarta or Rio de Janeiro.

In this context, it is worth asking whether the binary global North/global South continues to have relevance. In the 1990s, the terms 'global cities' and 'world cities' gained traction as geographers attempted to grapple with the increasing commonalities between cities worldwide. Abdoumaliq Simone argues that rather than seeing global South cities as dysfunctional colonial/post-colonial projects that are solely in need of better management and infrastructure, they should be considered as a frontier where people experiment with different forms of living, trading, and networking, in innovative, modern, and often resourceful ways. In Kinshasa, Democratic Republic of Congo, or Douala, Cameroon, Simone documents the dynamism with which the people make an alternative urban life, despite the impoverishment caused by structural inequalities. His focus is on the multitude of stories, strategies, emotions, and attitudes of urban inhabitants. Such a perspective might move the onlooker away from focusing solely on the potential for instability and violence that comes from deprivation.

A final form of segregation we might consider involves gender and sexual orientation. While urban life was perceived to give freedom from rural and provincial constraints, cities nevertheless reflected wider societal attitudes to gender and sexuality. Gender differences were built into the very infrastructure of modern cities. Skyscrapers have frequently been interpreted as phallic representation of masculine domination of the city. In urban planning, spaces considered to be public (male) and private (female) domains were designed into the built environment, notably during the period of suburbanization in North America and the UK from the 1930s onwards. In the 1970s, geographical studies of women's spatial behaviour focused on whether urban design enabled the efficient conduct of their domestic role as housewives by examining their mobility and access to shops and services. Later studies considered how attitudes that once excluded women from certain public spaces, coupled with the fear of violence outside the home, have been used to constrain their mobility in cities, especially at night. Since the 1970s, women in UK cities have protested the violence they experience in the public domain. The 'Reclaim the Night' movement, which started in 2004, has been a women-only march that occurs in UK cities against rape and all forms of male violence against women.

Infrastructural design focusing on women's domestic roles reinforced wider societal views that the nuclear heterosexual family was the norm, thus excluding those of lesbian, gay, bisexual, and transgender queer (LGBTQ+) communities. In response to discrimination, LGBTQ+ communities tended to create their own distinct urban spaces, which have been depicted as safe havens, but have not necessarily been so. Vulnerability to harassment is still experienced by those identifying as women, Black, transgender, and gender nonconforming. These queer spaces, such as West Village in New York, which were often located in deprived inner-city areas, have become gentrified or 'de-gayed', as an approved form of queer lifestyle has become appealing to mainstream consumption by heterosexuals as 'risqué' or 'fun'. Where sexuality and racial discrimination intersect, Black LGBTQ+ communities, for example, struggle to make their own liveable spaces as a marginalized group in an already marginalized community. This has become even more acute in cities where rent hikes and housing shortages are aggravated by precarious employment. In New York, queer youth, women of colour, and trans people had to form activist groups to contest gentrification and exclusion by white, often elderly, middle-class queers, while facing homophobic and transphobic violence from the outside world.

Cities at war

As seats of government and centres of economic activity, cities have long been targets of warfare. The history of urban sieges is a long and bloody one, lasting from the emergence of urban life all the way to the battles for Mariupol and Gaza City in the early 2020s. For millennia, cities were fortified, with city walls functioning both as defensive structures and means of filtering people as they entered the political community of the city in times of peace. Indeed, politics is derived from the Greek *politiká*, meaning the affairs of the city-state.

The advent of gunpowder had made city walls less effective against military invasions. The rise of aerial and nuclear warfare in the

20th century left cities and their populations even more vulnerable. Much of what happened to cities in the mid-20th century had to do with this new power to destroy. We have now almost become accustomed to seeing drone footage of urban ruins, be they in Syria or Ukraine. Geographers have spoken of vertical geopolitics to capture the multiple ways in which cities have been targeted and reorganized from above and below, from bunkers and panic rooms beneath West London 'iceberg' mansions to the satellite imagery used in the targeting of buildings and their inhabitants.

And indeed, individual structures do get caught up in war in a myriad ways. Think, for instance, of the Holiday Inn hotel, a yellow and brown tower built in the 1980s overlooking Sarajevo, a multicultural city in what is now Bosnia and Herzegovina, whose skyline is marked by minarets and church towers alike. When ethnic nationalism reared its head and (what was then) Yugoslavia descended into war, Sarajevo too came under attack. The siege, which began in 1993 and lasted for 1,425 days, turned the Holiday Inn into a crucial hotspot for and symbol of the urban population's suffering. It was here that politicians met to negotiate; it was here that journalists stayed to cover the war; and it was also here that sniper fire was at its most dangerous. And yet the staff kept the hotel going, serving breakfast, washing the bed linen, and dodging the sniper fire on their way to work. While some of the upper floors had to be cleared because they were exposed to fire, the staff kept up appearances by dressing formally. At one point, the company headquarters messaged to tell them it was okay to keep the hotel open, but asked them to kindly take the Holiday Inn sign down, which they feared was generating negative publicity for the brand given the amount of media exposure. The Sarajevo staff told them to drop by and take it down themselves. The sign, of course, stayed.

Although aerial bombardment against cities was pioneered in the First World War, it had no direct impact on the outcome of the war. Soon, however, bombers had extended their reach and payloads, making them virtually unstoppable. Although some anti-aircraft weapons had been developed and were deployed, they were not able to halt the bombing campaigns of the Second World War, which devastated urban centres in Europe and the Pacific, often striking urban populations indiscriminately in what we now know as carpet bombing. The two nuclear bombs dropped on Hiroshima and Nagasaki in August 1945 were in some ways simply a further development of the conventional bombing campaigns and similarly destructive to what had happened in Dresden or Tokyo, though the radiation did of course induce agonizing and often deadly mid- and long-term effects on its victims. But the successful testing of the thermonuclear weapon in the early 1950s meant that soon even major cities could be wiped off the map with a single bomb.

All of this resulted in changes to the way in which cities were built. After the Second World War, high-rise buildings were promised not just as a new way of housing the urban poor, but as a response to the threat of aerial bombardment. European and Japanese cities had burnt so well because the fire had spread so easily from block to block. Modern tower blocks promised more resilience. They were one of a range of ways in which cities were to be made survivable. But this too was short-lived. The two major Cold War superpowers soon had so many nuclear weapons in their arsenals, and the yields of these warheads were so much larger than those used in Hiroshima and Nagasaki, that even the large-scale construction of subterranean bunkers, which was attempted in some cities, was ultimately deemed futile.

And yet, the idea of resilience had a curious revival during the so-called war on terror of the 2000s. Attempts to redesign cities so that they were able to cope with terrorism more effectively sought to make urban space easier to police and more defensible. Like the city wall, planners tried to protect commercial activity while fortifying financial centres and shopping malls through more inconspicuous ways, via bollards and buffer zones and the increased use of CCTV. Rather than prompting a climate of fear by having too many guards with machine guns present in public life (although this did of course happen), a new anxious urbanism tried to remain just below the level of perceptibility, subtle and discreet.

Indeed, security and violence do not require armed struggle to find their way into the city. In the 21st century, gated communities and other privatized enclosures have spread globally, as urban elites segregate themselves in securitized compounds using private security companies and new surveillance technologies. Cities have become spaces in which surveillance and security manifest in repressive policing, which often features the tactics and weaponry used by the military.

Clearly, digital technology and artificial intelligence have transformed not only the home and workplace, but also urban planning. So-called smart cities have become increasingly popular. Security cameras on streets, front doors, facial recognition, drones, driverless cars, and intelligent buildings are some of the technological developments being encouraged under such schemes. Smart cities are promoted as representative of urban tech futures, and geographers have contributed to this transformation using Geographic Information Systems (GIS), digitally mapping areas that were previously unnavigable by public authorities, in particular informal settlements. Ayona Datta and Nancy Odendaal have tempered the enthusiasm for smart cities, pointing out how their promotion obscures power relations, especially in aspects of monitoring and controlling the urban population.

Chapter 5
The border

If you have ever attempted to climb a barbed wire fence
you will probably recall the sensation. Barbed wire punishes you
instantly for your transgression. It does so not at the level of
the law, but at that of the flesh.

Barbed wire and its cousin razor wire are used for a number
of purposes: to demarcate property, incarcerate and intern
people, and to secure territorial borders. The prevention of
movement is hardly the only way to exert power over bodies, but
it is a crucial one if we consider modern history. For the origins
of barbed wire lie in the 19th-century American West, where it
was initially used not on humans, but on cattle. Barbed wire
proved cheaper and more profitable and thus able to crowd out
earlier pastoral methods. But it cut across species. Humans too
soon got a taste of their own medicine.

Barbed wire fences proved effective, stealthy, and deadly on the
battlefields of the First World War. Barbs slowed the attackers
down and channelled them into unfavourable positions. They
were difficult to destroy, easy to replace, and almost impossible
to see at night. The sight of corpses caught in the wire was so
demoralizing that it was not uncommon for soldiers to risk their
lives to remove them from sight. The use of barbed wire proved
even more deadly in the network of concentration and death

camps which Nazi Germany constructed throughout its short-lived European empire. Indeed, fences were decisive and usually the first thing to go up when a camp was built. It was behind the wire that human beings could be killed—no longer as humans, but now as animals. The American plantation had never needed barbed wire because African slaves and their descendants were imprisoned by their phenotype. Fences were less central to the Soviet gulag too because the vast distances of northern Eurasia made an escape so difficult. But for a genocide of Europeans in densely populated Europe, fences were critical (Figure 10).

The idea that barbed wire could be used to demarcate territorial borders arrived late (Figure 11). An early border fence was built along the USA–Mexico border in the early 1900s. But half a century later, it divided an entire continent. The Berlin Wall was only the most visible stretch of 'iron curtain' that separated the Soviet and US spheres of influence during the Cold War. You may

10. **British soldiers carrying barbed wire picket posts along a communication trench, France 1916.**

11. Hungarian–Serbian border fence, constructed during Syrian refugee crisis in 2015.

have seen the iconic picture of an East German border guard jumping over some barbs during the Wall's construction in 1961. The image of this defecting soldier was used in the West to highlight that it was East Germany which was effectively imprisoning its citizens. This was true of course, but it was a convenient truth for the West which showed 'us' in the most favourable light, as a bastion of freedom, a place where people risked their lives to be.

In 1989, the Wall fell. It was brought down by peaceful protests and some confusion on the part of the East German regime. The Cold War had been winding down since the mid-1980s. Now it was over. People, goods, and ideas crossed the now defunct iron curtain. Other things seemed to be happening, too: new free trade agreements, the world wide web, the dissolution of the European Union's internal borders, and the rise of the 24-hour news cycle. The number of countries that did not have a McDonald's restaurant was rapidly decreasing. Territorial conflict and identity seemed to be losing their grip on everyday life. Many were quick to pronounce the dawn of a borderless world in which neoliberal globalization ruled supreme.

But the moment did not last. By the 2000s, it had become clear that something else was happening: re-borderization. The so-called war on terror in which the West engaged after the attacks of September 2001 prompted an explosion of a whole range of new bordering techniques. Russia had proved its willingness to resort to military means in the 2000s, but in 2014 it annexed the Crimean Peninsula and began a war in Eastern Ukraine. The 2010s also saw a violent anti-immigration politics previously confined to the far-right fringes of politics become normalized in the wider political landscape. The Syrian civil war moreover led to what was then the world's largest refugee crisis, in which more than 14 million Syrians were forced to flee their homes. In Europe, border fences went up to curb the influx of refugees. In the United States the 2016 presidential election was won by a candidate who promised to erect a wall on the USA–Mexico border. Reports of the death of borders had been greatly exaggerated.

Experiences of crossing borders can vary tremendously, depending on the kind of passports we possess and the types of borders we need to cross. Who gets to cross, who gets to stay, for how long, and with what legal rights, are key political issues of our time. And although we have a tendency to read the problem of the border through the prism of the ongoing struggle over migration, there is an older problem wrapped inside this question, that of territory.

Territory

Our discussion thus far has treated borders as historically contingent formations, which is to say that they come and go. But is it not *natural* for humans to demarcate territory? Animals, after all, display a whole range of territorial behaviours via sound, scent, as well as physical aggression. And are we humans not animals, too, one might ask?

The question is not new. It was the aforementioned zoologist turned geographer Friedrich Ratzel who claimed at the turn of the 20th century that states resembled organisms that struggled for space. The territorial border, he argued by analogy, was something of a peripheral organ (like the skin) which revealed the health of the organism as a whole. Growth was healthy and was achieved both via migration and military campaigns—but the organism went through a life cycle. Eventually, it would die, giving birth to other political organisms.

Ratzel's theory was deceptively simple and appealed to his contemporaries, who had become accustomed to looking to biology for ways to make sense of human societies. We may wonder, however, whether we would not see a different world, one with more divided cities and territorial conflicts, if territorial behaviour was indeed a biological urge, as Ratzel implied. Surely, there would be cities like Belfast and Nicosia all around us, more direct annexations like Russia's invasions of Ukraine, and more territories as parcelled up as the West Bank of Palestine. Divided cities are a captivating phenomenon, but, as we have noted, they are rare. Cities are more likely divided socio-economically than narrowly politically in terms of territorial allegiance, the often-cited examples of drug gangs or football supporters notwithstanding. True, a gated community is a bounded space—but it is not a sovereign territory. If the owner of a gated community in London tried to introduce capital punishment and administer executions, this would be illegal under British law, and they would face murder charges. While the proliferation of Special Economic Zones (SEZs) involves the handing over of some aspects of governance to corporations, the extent of their independence is still dependent on the power of national governments. Not all bounded spaces, in other words, are sovereign territories.

Territory is most frequently defined as a portion of the earth's surface which is claimed by a political group. We can find it on different scales, from sub-state (think of US federal states) to supranational (like the Schengen Area). Territory includes not just the two-dimensional area commonly depicted on political maps, but also the subsoil, internal and adjacent waters, as well as the airspace. It is, in other words, a 3D spatial container whose aim is to distinguish an inside from an outside. Territory matters as land, in the sense of ownership, and as terrain, in its military-strategic dimension. But ultimately it is hard to think of it outside the question of political authority and control. Indeed, the term's etymology reflects this multiple meaning. Territory's origins are ambivalent, stemming either from the Latin *terra* (for land or terrain) or from *territorium* (a place from which people are warned). The verb *terrere* means to frighten, which also highlights a possible link between territory and terror.

Rather than rendering territory as a basic instinct, it is perhaps more accurate to treat it as a political strategy, an attempt to exert influence by asserting control over a defined geographic area. This is referred to as 'territoriality'—and it does seem to capture something important about the relationship between power and space that is exerted through territory. It also begins to denaturalize territory, treating the latter less as an instinct than as a political tool. And yet, there is something missing here. For not all territorializations are conscious and deliberate acts.

Territory is also a learned behaviour. We are, for instance, taught a certain version of our history at school that privileges that which happened on the territory of 'our' state over that which happened elsewhere. Even children who have not yet encountered the question of territorial sovereignty in full will have a basic sense of 'their' territory from being exposed to mundane cartographic representations such as weather maps. Weather maps negotiate a sense of territorial belonging while navigating larger geopolitical questions. The BBC's weather map, for instance, does not

12. UK weather map.

include cities or temperature readings for the Republic of Ireland, though it does cover Northern Ireland. Note that while the BBC does not provide full information for mainland Europe either, it treats the 'British Isles' (thus including Ireland) as visually separate from the rest of the continent (see Figure 12). The choice is political. Full information for the Republic might invite the accusation that a former colony is still treated under the remit of the London-based BBC. Hungarian meteorologists have fewer qualms about including territories beyond the nation's recognized borders, particularly those areas with significant Hungarian populations. It is perhaps no coincidence that Hungarian weather maps thus realize the ultra-nationalist dream of a 'Greater Hungary'. West German weather maps displayed territories lost after the Second World War to Poland and the Soviet Union as German well into the 1970s.

What is more, some ages are noticeably more territorial than others. While it is rare today, territorial annexation was a frequent occurrence in the 19th century. This implies that territory cannot be timeless; it must have a history, and one which pre-dates that of barbed wire. Indeed, it is not just the distribution and ownership of territory which has changed over time, but the meaning of territory itself. Territory meant different things to the ancient Greeks or the Romans. For the Greeks, it was essentially the agricultural land around the city-state necessary to feed an urban population. The Roman empire's claim to universality made the idea of territory irrelevant. There were, to put it bluntly, areas controlled and others not yet controlled by Rome. Hard fortified borders, such as Hadrian's Wall, did exist, but they were the exception. The boundaries of the empire were fluid border zones. Even if they had wanted to establish territorial control in a modern sense, the Romans would not have had the cartographic tools to do so.

Medieval Europe was organized feudally. This was an order based on relationships between individuals rather than territorial entities, which makes it misleading to map medieval polities. It was only the rise of the modern state which gave birth to the current political map. Often, we read that the 1648 Treaties of Westphalia heralded the arrival of the modern state system. Indeed, the Westphalian peace enshrined principles into law which define the interstate system to this day, most notably the idea that each sovereign can determine domestic politics without fearing the intervention of another state. Religious denomination was the issue of the day: the idea that each new territorial state would be either Protestant or Catholic. If you did not like your state's religious preference, you could leave. Although the issue of denomination is not what states quarrel about today, the principle of sovereignty remains important in international law.

Westphalia did provide a solution to the problems of religious warfare that had raged through Europe in the decades preceding 1648. But it was not quite the historic break it is often seen as today. A system of separate and independent states with discrete territories had been in the making for centuries. Its birth prompted an explosion of cartographic activity. If states wanted territory, they needed to measure, demarcate, and represent it. But the birth of the modern state also went hand in hand with the colonial use of territory. Colonialism distinguished between states (mainly European powers) which were meant to respect each other's sovereignty and places (mainly though not exclusively outside Europe) that lacked sovereignty and that could be ruled colonially. English colonialism, moreover, had begun exerting its rule via the use of territorial space even before Westphalia. Ultimately, European colonialism exported not just methods of exploitation and a particular form of capitalism; it also spread the modern territorial state as a machine of demarcation. This, ultimately, is where geography as a recognizable field of knowledge originates.

Migration

Ten thousand years ago, humans were hunter gatherers who had to migrate to survive. Today, we are born into bounded nation-states that control our ability to move. Many of us cross borders for work and leisure. Others do so because they are fleeing war and persecution, because they wish for a better life, or because they are trafficked. Although we may be crossing the same borders, we might as well be inhabiting entirely separate universes.

Borders come in many shapes and forms. They exist in physical and symbolic form. Some are almost unnoticeable, others heavily militarized. There are maritime and land borders, unrecognized and so-called smart borders. Borders make use of geographical features, such as deserts and oceans and technology, from the simple border marker to a surveillance drone. But they also draw in bodies, those of border enforcement agents as much as those of the migrants. And borders are also of course omnipresent in the media landscape. The very categories of 'migrant' and 'asylum seeker' have become highly politicized.

Crossing a territorial boundary to a safe country was made an international human right for those fleeing persecution and war after the experiences of the Second World War. The understanding was that most refugees, especially those from global South countries, would return and start rebuilding their countries of origin once peace was achieved. This might have been the case until the 21st century; however, the number of protracted wars has grown and the international political will to resolve conflict seems to have waned post-Cold War. Consequently, the number of people seeking asylum and living with refugee status has increased globally. The United Nations Refugee Agency put the figure at 108.4 million people in 2022, after 5.7 million Ukrainians and 4.4 million, mainly Afghans and Venezuelans, were added that year.

It was as recent as 2007 that, according to Bastian A. Vollmer, 'the first piece of UK parliamentary legislation carrying the word border received royal assent'. Since then, the term has become ubiquitous in public discourse. News portals are filled with talk of 'our borders', 'wide open borders', 'waves', and 'invasions'. Migrants and refugees have often been depicted as criminals and dehumanized in other and even more serious ways. Host governments, especially those in the global North, have made the act of seeking asylum increasingly difficult, even though the bulk of refugees remain in global South countries. This has had serious implications, such as increasing people's vulnerability to human trafficking. Although 145 states have signed up to the 1951 Refugee Convention, the right to asylum is steadily eroded.

Borders are the place, not the only but a crucial one, where we have to identify ourselves to authority, by showing our passport, if we have one. The state derives much of its authority from the filtering of flows into and out of its territory. Rather than thinking of borders as discrete boundaries which delimit one state's jurisdiction from another, it can be more useful to think of bordering as a practice, an active doing that needs to be repeated over and over again to produce the state itself. Borders order. And they do so not just at the physical border, but far beyond. Communities that inhabit borderlands experience the spillover of border policing into the mainland. Schools, universities, employers, and landlords are today all drafted into the border regime. Anywhere you are asked to identify yourself, the border in a sense opens up. This has served in places as a blueprint for racist treatment of different kinds. And if you have the wrong passport or your visa has run out, then things can get ugly pretty quickly.

Drawing borders has often featured violence. Sustaining borders usually entails further violence. Along the USA–Mexico border 686 died or disappeared in 2022 alone, making it the world's deadliest land route for migrants. Some are killed directly by border agents, but the majority die because modern technology has made their journeys so treacherous. The use of drones, motion and heat sensors, armoured vehicles, and helicopters has blurred the boundary between the military and police dimensions of national security. The US Customs and Border Protection agencies are allowed to operate within 100 miles of the border and remain almost unaccountable. In 2020, they were also drawn on to police the racial justice protests even though there was no obvious connection to their mandate.

States have not always cared so much about migration as they do today. The United States had become more interested in distinguishing their own citizens from those of other states in the late 19th century after a wave of anti-immigration discourse swept through the country. Some of the first immigration acts in the USA and Canada were introduced to curb the inflow of Chinese migrants and Jewish refugees. In Europe, you could still walk from Lisbon to Moscow without having to show a passport until the First World War. Once states had decided to try to control immigration, documentation became necessary. Increasingly, populations were managed and monitored via border patrols and customs agents. It was in the early 20th century that an initial form of biometric technology was introduced—the fingerprint, first used by the British colonial state to control populations in India.

The aim of the modern border is to distinguish 'legal' from 'illegal' migrant, 'citizen' from 'non-citizen'. Those who are seen to contribute to the economy are welcome, others are not. In the wake of the war on terror and the tightening of border regimes in the global North, borders have become increasingly sophisticated at monitoring and filtering movement across borders at a whole range of scales. Those who pass through major airports have become accustomed to self-checkouts that use facial or iris recognition, biometric forms of control which in effect inscribe the border onto our bodies. Only very few will experience what lies beyond. Although journalists do not have access to migrant detention centres, UK newspapers have reported that access to health care is extremely difficult, and rooms may feature shared toilets with no curtain to draw. There is violence. Unlike in prisons, migrants can be detained indefinitely with severe impact on their mental health.

Beyond such internal practices, there is a geographically ever more sophisticated array of external border practices, chiefly out-sourcing and offshoring. Many countries in the global North now police borders remotely by funding countries in the global South to help manage their borders. This follows similar policies in the realm of the prison system. In 2015, the United Kingdom, for instance, announced that it was building a prison in Jamaica for £25 million in an attempt to move prisoners from UK prisons. It is worth noting that both prisons and immigration detention centres are often run for profit by the same companies. This is a reminder that the basic function of the restriction of movement, once done so effectively with the use of barbed wire, tends to attract similar political agents and spatial formations. The consequence is what Alison Mountz calls the 'enforcement archipelago', sprawling and dispersed sets of infrastructures, sites, policies, and people whose aim it is to geographically distance migrants from the nation-state and its territory.

Human mobility has been essential to the well-being of human society and for economic growth in capitalist economies. Particularly in the ageing societies of the global North, an in-flow of labour migrants is vital to ensure continued economic growth. Given these pressures, governments realize that closing borders to migrants is unrealistic and instead seek to exert a tighter rein on who can enter, for what duration, and who cannot. In doing so, they seek to cater to a rising hostility towards migrants.

The violence of bordering practices has encouraged human geographers to adapt border abolition as an approach to thinking about what mobility justice might look like. Noting the racial differences in states' approaches to people who move, they draw on the prison abolition movement of African Americans campaigning against the high incarceration rate of Blacks, Latinos, and Native Americans in the USA. Their struggle is not so much about abolishing borders per se, but about transforming the conditions in countries of origin, so that people have the freedom to move or stay, and to ensure just migrant policies where everyone has the freedom to move without being detained or deported.

The return of the border

The old colonial distinction of a world in which sovereignty must be respected, and one where it does not, lives on today. But the persistence of border wars, of wars for territory, does not mean that territory is timeless. The world has seen moments of deterritorialization, including that following the dissolution of the Soviet sphere of influence in 1991. If territory was natural rather than cultural, then we should see it play a role in all societies throughout history.

The idea that we live in an era marked by the demise of borders was long a cliché in debates about globalization. It has now become very clear that the opposite is true. The experience of borders concerns us all, either because we are migrants or because our ancestors were. Whether secured by barbed wire, passports, drones, or satellites, territory can be understood as a strategy of establishing power through the construction of closed space. But it is important to remember that there is only so much that can be achieved by closing off space. During the 2020 Covid-19 pandemic, states showed that they could exert their power by closing territorial borders. But they could only contain the virus in some cases and for comparatively limited periods of time. Even the most fortified state of all, North Korea, was not able to insulate itself from the virus.

In the early 21st century, territorial borders, including those policed in cyberspace, remain important loci of political struggles, not least because they have retained that original violence which the existence of territory was once meant to expel. This raises the question of whether there are any alternatives to a territorial exercise of political power in the world today. One such alternative is proposed by the border abolition movement, which was motivated by the movements to abolish prisons and, before that, slavery. It may be easy to cast border abolitionists as utopians, not least in the current political climate, as people with a good sense of what they are against but not what they are for. But like the prison system and slavery, the border needs to be seen as an institution built upon the deeper foundations of racism, capitalism, and the nation-state, all of which divide, categorize, and exclude; the border is the place where such injustices materialize in perhaps the starkest form.

Chapter 6
The workplace

Every day, on almost every street in the countries of the global North, vans, bicycles, and motorbikes deliver online purchases, especially consumer goods and takeaway meals (Figure 13). Traversing the same streets may be drivers who use their private cars as taxis for ride-hailing companies like Uber. Subjected to tight work schedules, these drivers and riders are often criticized for being reckless. They are at the forefront of consumer anger and vulnerable to unprovoked attacks from the public, a public which paradoxically has come to rely on the swiftness of their services.

What we know as the workplace has changed significantly in the early 21st century. Mobile workplaces are representative of the gig economy—a labour market where people work in jobs that are flexible, freelance, short-term, and where workers cannot rely on the legal protection and rights often associated with a permanent job, such as holiday, sick, or maternity pay. Even where the workplace is in a fixed location, such as a distribution warehouse or a supermarket, workers may be employed on casual, precarious contracts with no stated working hours. In the UK these are known as 'zero-hour contracts'. Such job insecurity, exacerbated by the recent advent of artificial intelligence, means that we no longer live by the dictum of a 'job for life'.

13. **Uber Eats delivery cyclist in Manchester.**

Over the last half-century, work—the activity that produces gainful outcomes that are life sustaining—has become a key focus of geographical interest. How could it not be? Work and the workplace are widely seen as important to economic growth, to urbanization and development, to the reproduction of family life, and to the constitution of our identities. Work defines who we are and how we live our lives. It profoundly shapes our life trajectories as well as our everyday movements across space and time.

In the summer of 1968, a group of sewing machinists staged a strike. The women, whose job it was to make car seats for the Ford motor factory in Dagenham on the outskirts of London, were fed up that they were being paid significantly less than their male peers for the same work. Their struggle for equal pay, depicted in the 2010 feature film *Made in Dagenham*, garnered widespread attention, and their case was taken on by the then Employment Secretary Barbara Castle and ultimately resulted in the 1970 Equal Pay Act, a piece of legislation designed to prohibit discrimination as regards terms and conditions of employment between men and women. The striking workers gained a small pay rise, not equal pay, and in 1984, the women at Ford went on strike again.

Part of the problem was that women's labour was deemed to be no more than supplementary to men's. In a seminal 1978 article, Jacqueline Tivers questioned geographical research that classified households according to the work of the male breadwinner and thus ignored women's individual experience and contribution. She states, 'it is this concentration on the family role of the woman, and especially on her role as a mother, which largely determines both the woman's position in society and her lack of worth as an object of serious academic attention'.

For long, work has been assumed to be an activity that occurs in specific designated sites, be they factories, offices, farms, construction, or retail sites; the home as a workplace and child rearing as work have been overlooked. Tivers's provocation was influential in encouraging geographers to examine gender inequalities in a wider set of geographical spaces and to look deeper into household dynamics to understand how the disproportionate responsibility that women hold for childbearing and rearing still has an impact on their pay. Half a century after the sewing machinists walked out at Dagenham, the UK's gender pay gap, the difference between the average wage of men and women in the same workplace, remains high at 14.3 per cent. Even with the increased workplace and work time flexibility associated with the contemporary gig economy, women still earn less than men due to the time spent on unpaid caring responsibilities and domestic labour.

The continued gendered distribution of domestic and caring responsibilities became particularly obvious when in 2020 homes were turned into remote workplaces as a response to government measures to combat the Covid-19 pandemic. Globally, women were more likely to lose their job during Covid than men, and they were also more likely to forgo paid work because they were caring for others. The ability to work at home during Covid was dependent on a whole range of factors such as occupation, housing, as well as different national furlough schemes. The pandemic also exposed the racialized inequalities of work in the global North, especially when death rates among low-paid key workers from immigrant groups were higher than the white population. At the same time, workers in the global South whose jobs were reliant on Northern consumer markets were made unemployed, often without any form of compensation.

Within capitalist societies, the common assumption is that the location of workplaces emerges from the decisions of what 19th-century economists termed 'economic man', an imagined figure that sought to respond 'rationally' to market drivers, the forces of demand and supply. But the events from Dagenham to Covid-19 shine a different light on the geography of work. The epoch-making shift of manufacturing to countries in the global South is underpinned by cultural and racial assumptions about the value of work in different world regions, resulting in an international division of labour. Historically, not all workplaces have been characterized by voluntary labour. Even in the 21st century, some are still forced to work under modern slavery—a figure the United Nations estimated on any day in 2021 to be 27.6 million. Even where workers are 'free', there is a constant struggle for better working conditions and living wages.

Location!

Economic geographers have long examined why companies relocate to particular places. Doreen Massey was amongst the first to explore how the geographical distribution of workplaces is closely linked to the wider social structure of a society—specifically how it is shaped by class, gender, and racial ideology. Using the UK as an example, she showed how the historical concentration of high-status white-collar jobs in London and the South-East, and heavy industrial working-class jobs in South Wales and the North of England, produced a 'spatial division of labour' that reflected wider social and cultural differences in British society, which in turn influenced government policies and location decisions. Higher-status jobs had greater leverage within firms and thus greater ability to shape strategic decisions. Areas where working-class jobs predominated were more likely to be affected by economic restructuring, including deindustrialization, because lower-status workers had less social power in firms and less influence on government.

Massey stressed that the UK's spatial division of labour was not universal. Indeed, each country has a different social and economic history that affects its spatial division of labour. Her pioneering work shifted geographical thinking to recognize the influences of a combination of factors—economic, political, social, and cultural—that affect where economic activities take place. In addition to individual entrepreneurs, corporations, and banks, institutions such as the state, development agencies, and NGOs all influence where economic activities occur. These actors all operate with different interests and changing assumptions about the workforce. Think about the incentives a government might offer a company to set up a factory in an area of high unemployment. Consequently, where work is located changes over time and is characterized by geographical unevenness and social inequality.

In many countries of the global North, we can find regions that were once pulsating centres of industrial activity, but are now subject to deindustrialization. There are also regions characterized by new knowledge-based economic activities, such as Silicon Valley in California, home to many IT and high-tech companies. At the same time, we can observe the persistence of certain economic activities in cities, particularly the service sector. Think of financial districts like the City of London or New York's Wall Street, where wealth is highly concentrated. The geographer

David Harvey has provided an explanation for this spatial pattern of unevenness. He argues that the spatial restlessness of economic activities and the resultant inequalities between places are the consequences of capitalism trying to resolve its inherent problems. Capitalism is crisis prone. Conditions that produce crises vary, but a common one is when there is a surplus of labour and money and limited ways of putting them into profitable activities. Looking back in history, we can identify economic crises in the 1870s, 1930s, 1970s, 1990s, and, more recently, the financial crisis of 2007–8. Some attempts to adjust economies to address these crises may have only short-term successes; more substantive changes involve restructuring, which tends to have geographical and social consequences, as with deindustrialization above.

History has shown us that capitalism requires constant technological and geographical expansion to maintain continuous economic growth. Harvey contends that globalization has its roots in the 15th-century European quest for gold and other commodities in the Americas. On a more abstract level, it was the symptom of capitalism's eternal quest for a 'spatial fix' to its tendency towards crisis. Peter Dicken has mapped out how continued capitalist globalization has produced a geography of production, distribution, and consumption on a worldwide scale. Technological change, enabling the mobility of raw materials and commodities from producers to consumers (e.g. shipping containers and communication systems), has generated complex global production networks over time, in which producers and consumers are linked through sequences of interdependent activities that span the globe. In the late 20th-century phase of globalization, the ease of flows of money and goods has been enabled by global institutions such as the World Trade Organization and the International Monetary Fund, regional economic unions such as the European Union and the North American Free Trade Agreement, as well as individual nation-states using neoliberal economic doctrines which aim to unleash the power of the free market and remove protectionist regulatory frameworks such as trade tariffs.

In effect, globalization has been reliant on the creation of distinct workplaces across the globe which cater to specific social relations that differentiate between human needs. Following Cedric Robinson, human geographers have recognized the role of racial ideology in European society, even prior to the emergence of modern capitalism. An example of this is the persecution and expulsion of Jews and Muslims from Spain and Portugal during the late 15th century and the papal bulls that provided religious justification for the differential treatment of non-Catholics. Such views were then carried beyond Europe's shores with the onset of colonialism and became enshrined in a new economic order. Since the capitalist economic system utilized racism as the basis of profit generation from its very inception, it is therefore best described as 'racial capitalism'. Race, in other words, is at the very heart of modern capitalism and thus shapes how modern workplaces are constituted.

Gender and race in the workplace

In the late 1970s, feminist geographers recognized that women had been missing from the study of the economy, labour, and work. They began to challenge the assumption that women's work was peripheral to the economy by showing how and where women were in fact incorporated into the workforce. Gendered stereotypes abounded with expectations about what kind of work men and women were expected to perform. Crucial amongst these was a widespread form of dualist thinking that associated work and the public sphere with men and home and the private sphere with women, a binary construction which discriminated against women and ignored their contribution to the economy.

Massey's pioneering work considered how the job status of employees was related to their gender. She showed how industries such as mining relied on and strengthened societal conceptions of masculinity, by associating certain skills with men, and how the social interpretations placed on 'paid work' could themselves shape certain gender categories. Even today, many jobs are implicitly classified according to whether they are 'men's jobs' or 'women's jobs'. Even after equality legislation was introduced and more women entered the labour market, gender still plays a crucial role. Linda McDowell's work has shown that wherever economic restructuring has resulted in the demise of manufacturing jobs, working-class men have tended to feel that their masculinity is threatened. These men, she reveals, had been socialized into believing that they must undertake tough, back-breaking work, which disqualifies them from most service sector jobs (e.g. hospitality, retail) that require soft/feminine skills. Working-class masculinity is different from the supposed 'cerebral masculinity' that middle-class men practise in their higher-status jobs. Both forms of masculinity, and many hybrid forms, continue to be performed in many workplaces whether on the factory floor, in the mines, in investment banks, in corporate boardrooms, or in fast food restaurants, and are present in dress codes as much as in the allocation of senior roles in a given company.

McDowell argues that the rise of service economies has led to increased focus on the individual bodies of workers, especially in the more interactive customer-facing service sector in the UK and USA, where there is direct interaction between the worker and the consumer, as in waitressing and hairdressing. She states that the physical attributes of the bodies providing services are part of the commodity that is being bought and thus the economic exchange. Most forms of employment have long rewarded or expected well-groomed, slim bodies. Skin colour, weight, disability, and perceived cultural attractiveness have become increasingly important in the differentiated labour market. Work in the home or away from customers can be outsourced to those with physical features considered less favourable.

Industrialization within the capitalist system separated spaces of production from spaces of reproduction. Earlier feminist geography challenged the view that women's reproductive activities (nurturing of the family) are non-economic and traced the importance of gender in the spatial restructuring of economic activities. Natalie Oswin has revealed how the nuclear, heterosexual family has been promoted globally as the ideal/proper modern social unit with clearly defined gender roles that constitute respectable domesticity. Such perspectives have informed states and development agencies' undermining of other family forms, such as the extended families in global South cultures and single-parent and queer families. In much of the global South, the neglect of female domestic labour has extended to all women's work, whether it be farming for domestic consumption, trading, the sale of crop surpluses and cooked food, or the home sewing of clothes under formal/informal contracts. Even today, these forms of work are seen as supplementing male household income and signs of female empowerment outside the public sphere. However, at certain conjunctures—times of severe labour shortages and during wars—women have been brought into the formal labour force and subjected to working conditions not dissimilar to men.

We have already discussed how racism enables the unequal differentiation of human value. However, the specific characteristics of racial capitalism have been noted to vary from one part of the capitalist world to another, depending on societal histories and peopling. During the era of European colonialism, where wealth had to be extracted directly from the earth (e.g. precious metals) or produced through agricultural production (sugar, cotton), workers were needed. This labour shortage became more acute where Indigenous peoples inhabiting colonized lands were decimated by disease brought by Europeans or where they had already been few. Europeans' use of enslaved peoples started with the Portuguese in Ceuta after they conquered it in the 15th century and was later expanded by the British on the Caribbean island of Barbados to produce sugar for UK consumers after attempts to use white indentured workers from Britain had failed. The Barbados Slave Code of 1661 was the first legal instrument produced to codify slavery. Here, Black African people were described as 'a heathenish, brutish, and uncertain dangerous kind of people', whose rights where curtailed so that they could be treated as personal property or chattel. Dehumanization enabled the commodification and enslavement of African people and their transportation across the Atlantic Ocean and sale to white men who used their labour growing crops (largely sugar and cotton) on plantations. Europeans classified the peoples according to race and used such racial categories to create distinct economic entities, of which the plantation was an early one.

Katherine McKittrick maps out the geographical sites of bondage that accompanied slavery, most crucially the slave ship, the auction block, the coffle (a chained line of slaves), and, of course, the plantation. As a workplace, the plantation utilized racism as the basis of profit generation and was supported by the political system of colonialism. Some of the first plantations were constructed in Ireland, where Queen Elizabeth I expropriated land from the Irish and gave it to English settlers. Best known are the slave plantations in South and North America and the Caribbean. These capitalist spatial forms were considered ideal for the industrial-like production of agricultural goods and have been replicated across the world in tea, coffee, and palm oil estates in Asia and the land concessions given to transnational companies for mining and rubber production.

As a workplace, the slave plantation in the Americas and the Caribbean was a space of extreme capitalist exploitation where ideas of racialization were perfected (Figure 14). It was a space of domination and differentiation with a distinct labour hierarchy designed to enable large-scale capitalist agricultural production in a controlled setting. Embodied plantation work was determined

14. Romanticized depiction of cotton plantation, 1840.

by race and skin colour gradations. The owners and foremen were of course racialized as white. Enslaved Black people worked in the fields and those with lighter skin tones—most likely the products of rape—often worked in the house of the white slave master. As enslaved peoples had no value beyond the utility of their labour, plantations were sites of subjection, brutality, and pain. Forced procreation, prohibition of marriages, and separation of parents and children deprived enslaved peoples of familial bonds. On the plantation, enslaved people became commodities to which prices were attached. As embodied property, they could be bought and sold and subjected to terror at the whim of the slave-owning class.

Since its inception, the spatial arrangement of the sugar, coffee, and cotton plantations of the Americas has been echoed in other spatial forms such as in racially segregated colonial towns elsewhere in the world. While the British Emancipation Act of 1833 abolished slavery in the Caribbean, thus removing the legal right of plantation owners to chattel ownership of people, labour exploitation persisted with the apprenticeship system enforced on formerly enslaved peoples for a further eight years. Indian indentured workers were recruited and transported to work on plantations in the British colonies of Trinidad and Tobago, Fiji, and Guyana and to build the railways in East and South Africa. Chinese labourers were recruited to South-East Asia and the Caribbean. The working conditions of indentured workers were only marginally better than those of enslaved peoples.

The demise of slavery in the Americas did not eliminate the racialized economic exploitation that had proliferated in the colonies. With varying degrees of coercion, it persists today, particularly in sites of resource extraction. The era of the plantation endures too, of course, in the form of large-scale monocropping (e.g. oil palm, tea, and banana plantations), with varying degrees of labour exploitation.

The international division of labour

What can we say about recent trends in the geography of labour? As we have seen, post-1970s globalization has shifted industrial production from global North countries to those in the global South. While countries such as China were able to emerge as global manufacturing hubs, global North countries became centres of research and consumption. This arrangement has meant cheaper goods and services for global North consumers. Earlier, we also saw how deindustrialization in the global North affected gendered identities. Not surprisingly, new production sites in the South have relied on racial, gendered, and cultural assumptions about local workers and their capacity to endure inhumane conditions.

Fast fashion, the production of clothes that are based on trends and easily disposable, is a particularly instructive example to get a glimpse of what is going on in the globalized production network. The industry is heavily criticized for its environmental impact and for the conditions under which the clothes are produced. In November 2012, a fire in the nine-storey Tazreen Fashion factory, on the outskirts of the capital city of Dhaka in Bangladesh, killed some 112 people. Six months later, again on the outskirts of Dhaka, an eight-storey building containing five garment factories collapsed, killing 1,133 workers, and injuring 2,500. These were workplaces sewing fast fashion for major retail companies headquartered in the global North that had outsourced production to factories in the global South. The problem comes down to practices designed to keep costs low. This is done in several ways, either by violating international labour standards or by devaluing workers' rights, particularly through international agreements allowing companies to operate in urban areas demarcated in some parts of the world, such as China, as export-processing Special Economic Zones (SEZs). SEZs are normally exempt from national legislations relating to minimum pay and health and safety in the workplace. Following the disasters in Dhaka, it took a global public outcry, consumer pressure on retailers, and local union campaigns for Bangladesh to introduce new legislation aimed at improving working conditions.

That the majority of workers who died in these two tragedies were young women is hardly surprising. As we have seen, job segmentation in the workplace defines what types of work are suitable for men and women. Low-skilled and repetitive work, tasks such as sewing in textile factories, is commonly seen as more suitable for women. Young female workers from farming backgrounds are viewed by states and employers as the most docile and exploitable workers. In China, according to C. Cindy Fan, these women, who are known locally as *dagongmei* (working young women), tend to be rural to urban migrants, who are provided housing in factory dormitories and who, due to government restrictions on residency in urban areas, are expected to eventually return to their rural homes.

The labour geographer Madhumita Dutta highlights the everyday experiences of migrant workers and the choices they make in moving to work in these urban-based factories in India. Some young female workers hope to break free from the gender restrictions in their patriarchal rural communities and generate income that will allow them a degree of independence before conforming to societal expectations of marriage and domesticity. In some contexts, waged work in factories, despite its precarity and exploitation, can allow women to escape or negotiate more oppressive home situations.

Poor women from the global South, even those married and with children, have increased their participation in transnational labour migration flows, as new and flexible workplace opportunities have opened up in global North economies. Transnational domestic workers, whether they be Filipinos in Hong Kong, Indonesians and Africans in the Gulf states, or Latinos in North America, have become a feature of many economies. In 2019, the International Labour Organization estimated that there were some 5.83 million domestic workers in six Gulf countries. Transnational migrant workers are recruited to the care industries catering for the ageing global North demographics and flown in to do seasonal agricultural work. Since the early 2000s New Zealand dairy farms have relied on temporary workers from mainly the Philippines, Fiji, and India. Similar schemes exist in Canada, Australia, the USA, and the UK. Such work is presented as win-win for the receiving and sending countries, but such optimism is clouded by reports of broken contracts followed by forced repatriation, indebtedness to recruitment companies, virtual imprisonment of workers, and lack of benefits even when paying local taxes. Care and farm work breaks down even further the dichotomy between the home and the workplace. Working conditions in private homes and farms are shielded from the scrutiny of unions and can be spaces where the violent abuse of workers, especially women, goes unnoticed (Figure 15).

15. Migrant workers protesting in Hong Kong.

In many countries, SEZs and the gig economy are reliant on non-unionized precarious workers, raising the question to what extent these workers are able to mobilize for better working conditions and wages. Historically, with the exception of communist China, labour unions have been responsible for the achievement of improved occupational health and safety conditions in workplaces and better wages. Since the 1970s, however, with the rise of a neoliberal, free-market approach to the economy, unions have been represented as a hindrance to growth. Collective bargaining for improved pay and conditions is still the main option available for the majority of workers. Yet, there is the question as to the degree to which workers are indeed able to make a difference in the workplace, particularly in an era characterized by labour migration and outsourcing. The online retailer Amazon and the ride-sharing company Uber long refused to recognize union membership for their warehouse and delivery staff and drivers respectively. Unionization or collective bargaining have occurred only in specific locations after worker activism and successful legal claims in courts. Workers in global production networks, where ownership and nodes in the networks are transparent, have shown the potential to mobilize transnationally for improved wages and conditions.

In the 21st century, human geographers have played an important role in making sense of the spatial and structural inequalities in the workplace, especially the global shifts that have created new forms of economic precarity in former industrial regions of the world, while enabling prosperity in others. Persistent unemployment and grievances amongst working-class communities in the global North have led to questions about the political feasibility of globalization processes that fuel ideological oppositions, as seen in the rise of far-right political movements and politicians across the globe and the primacy of a politics that is more narrowly defined by the so-called national interest. The political class in the USA and Europe has been startled not just by Russia's anti-liberal coalition, but also by the Chinese Belt and Road initiative and intensifying forms of South–South Cooperation. As geopolitics returns as a key force in economic decision-making, there is likely to be further global economic restructuring and shifts of manufacturing workplaces back to the global North or to politically aligned states. This may explain the promotion and expansion of SEZs/freeports in the global North, as well as in Central America and Africa.

Chapter 7
The conservation area

In 2015, a lion nicknamed Cecil was killed by an American dentist whom photographs would later depict as a man with sparkly white teeth and big smile. Walter Palmer had paid US $54k to trophy hunt Cecil in Hwange National Park, Zimbabwe. As a well-fed park lion accustomed to contact with humans, Cecil was hardly difficult to kill. The big cat was shot at short range by bow and arrow. But Palmer had missed the animal's vital organs. Possibly because he wanted to register the kill as a bow-hunted specimen, the dentist waited and left the wounded animal to suffer for hours before finally deciding to finish it off.

Cecil's killing sparked an unprecedented outcry. The lion had been GPS tagged as part of a research project carried out by academics of Oxford University. Soon, a single dead African animal was gaining more global attention than all the wars and uprisings raging on the continent put together. Conservation NGOs were quick to jump on the chance that the death of this animal offered. This raised questions about the commodification of wildlife and the emotions generated in the West by charismatic species. It shed light too on the ways in which conservation groups use the spectre of trophy hunting to generate income. What got lost in the ensuing debate, however, was the fact that while a wealthy American could pay to slay a lion, local people living in the area were not allowed to kill these animals, even if their lives were threatened.

The above incident illustrates how conservation policy is set largely in the global North by academics, international NGOs, and multilateral institutions. The 'Cecil Summit', held in Oxford in 2016, brought together a range of actors to set the agenda for lion conservation in Africa. The problem for the attendees was not so much wealthy tourists killing animals to generate revenue for parks, but rural Africans eking out a living on the land. Seen as the main threat to wildlife, they tend to be labelled 'poachers' who are vulnerable to being shot on sight as conservation has become increasingly securitized and militarized. Poaching for rhino horns and elephant tusks is a lucrative illegal business. And although it is driven by international demand, the term 'poaching' has been used to criminalize all unofficial African activities in protected areas. Poachers are, in more than one sense, an easy target.

Although there is significant variation across countries, nature conservation is generally characterized by the attempt to create safe spaces for non-humans. Conservation relies on a geographical device, invariably known as protected area, national park, forest and nature reserve, site of special scientific interest, nature conservancy, or conservation area (not to be confused with architectural protection areas). Such spaces seek to regulate human and non-human behaviour by a range of means, including most importantly by physical and virtual demarcation: markers, fences, GIS systems, GPS location, and a whole range of legal tools. The scale of such operations is not insignificant. In 2018, around 15 per cent of the world's land surface was in an internationally protected area, and not without reason. The dynamics of global warming and habitat loss have resulted in staggering biodiversity loss. The International Conservation Union (IUCN) estimates in 2023 that around 26 per cent of the world's mammal species face extinction. Scientists speak of a 'sixth global mass extinction'. Many see protected areas as a cornerstone policy for keeping extinction at bay.

What often gets missed in accounts of conservation is its human geography, for modern conservation emerged and still stands at the interface of science and colonialism. In 2020, the geographer William M. Adams wrote that 'Geographers have long recognized that conservation, as a social and political practice, is fundamentally spatial'. Its main strategy is the demarcation of spaces as protected areas within which rules control what humans (and non-humans) do.' In many cases, the establishment of conservation was accompanied by the forced removal of Indigenous peoples from these newly created protected areas. The British colonial Game Ordinance of 1940, for example, restricted new settlement in the area that in 1957 became the Serengeti National Park and Ngorongoro Conservation Area in Tanzania. Across much of South and South-East Asia, forest reserves were created to turn wilderness into a resource. Many contemporary protected areas were overlaid onto these colonial entities. Since the 1960s, international organizations, such as the IUCN, have been campaigning to restrict human activity in Serengeti and Ngorongoro, and have lobbied the independent Tanzanian government to remove Maasai pastoralists from the Serengeti who have lived in these areas for millennia. Forced removals have continued into the 21st century, with 3,000 evicted at gunpoint in 2009 and plans to remove a further 150,000 Maasai put in place in 2022 amidst protests. This case poses two interrelated questions: who benefits from conservation, and whose perspective of nature is being conserved?

Inhuman geographies

Conservation is generally thought of as an endeavour that benefits nature and humankind. And it does of course. But often, conservation policies and practices which target the global public underplay or ignore the politics of conservation, that is, the unequal power relations underlying decision-making on what to conserve. This politics plays out over and through the demarcation of space—but it is also fought out in the very language we use. The phrase 'human impact on the environment' connotes a universal human, whose action is the same everywhere. But recent research on climate change and biodiversity loss indicates the differential impacts of human action across the globe and the role economic systems play in degradation and increasingly in determining how best to conserve the environment. These unequal geographies of responsibility for planetary degradation reflect the North–South divide explored in our discussion of development and the racial legacies of colonialism.

Since the establishment of royal hunting grounds in Europe, protected areas have been carved out and maintained for the enjoyment of elites at the exclusion of others. Over time, such spaces gained widespread approval if they were represented as being for the benefit of a much wider public and for future generations. Similar spaces were carved out in settler colonial contexts. National parks are usually said to originate in the United States with the establishment of Yellowstone National Park, which was founded in 1872 by presidential decree—the consequence of lobbying by environmental activists appalled by industrial pollution and public misuse. The Park was to be set aside for public enjoyment and to conserve flora and fauna, a noble aim for sure. But for this to happen, the 27 Indigenous communities who lived in the 8,991km area were forcibly displaced and prohibited from carrying out their livelihood activities, such as hunting and fishing. From the very beginning, conservation was thus underwritten by colonial violence.

In the 21st century, conservation is a busy field which attracts not just charities and NGOs, but also politicians, explorers, and actors in the global North. Such celebrities are widely used to front environmental campaigns. Imaginative geographies promoted by children's books and anthropomorphic films, such as Walt

Disney's *The Lion King*, have played a key role in popularizing global environmental narratives and campaigns. So too have charismatic species, large or small. Pandas, lions, elephants, rhinos, orangutans, and koalas are used to rally public support in conservation campaigns and to attract financial donations. Of course, what is charismatic in the global North may not be charismatic in the communities in the global South.

According to Dan Brockington and Katherine Scholfield, philanthropic donations have grown, generating numerous new international NGOs. Saving nature has become a business. They use the term 'conservationist mode of production' to describe the ways in which conservation NGOs in Africa promote and spread capitalist solutions to environmental problems. Since the 1980s, neoliberal economic solutions have framed the environment as a set of assets that can be priced and traded on the market like other goods. If aspects of nature have become private property (belonging to nations, Indigenous communities, or individuals in the case of game ranchers), then, as with other forms of property, efforts are made to keep them secure from theft. Today, this involves increasing the securitization and militarization of conservation areas: wardens are given military training and guns and equipped with shoot-to-kill policies so they can target poachers. Western audiences and city-dwelling Indigenous elites, who might be sympathetic to this view, like to downplay or ignore the number of people killed by wild animals or shot because they are mistaken for poachers. In Tanzania alone, a 2005 study found that lions had killed 563 humans over a 25-year period.

Geographers critical of the exclusionary conservation practices in the global South coined the term 'fortress conservation' to capture the way in which modern conservation encourages the establishment of enclosures that are set aside exclusively for nature and for tourist encounters by largely global North elites. Militarized conservation is also visible at a larger scale.

The case of the Chagos Islanders and Diego Garcia illustrates how geopolitical relations can allow a protected area to come into being despite moral justifications against it. In 1966 the British government signed a lease with Washington for the Indian Ocean island of Diego Garcia. The island was to be used as a joint UK/US military base and the inhabitants were forcedly displaced between 1968 and 1973. When, in 2010, it appeared that the islanders' 40-year campaign to return might be successful, British and American politicians and military personnel met to create the world's largest marine protected area—640,000km^2—encompassing the archipelago. Promoted by conservationists as the most important marine reserve in the world, all fishing, including sustainable fishing, which would have been the livelihood activity of the Chagossians, was banned. Elizabeth de Santo and others argue that this decision was taken without sufficient scientific evidence to justify the 'no-take' restrictions. In effect, it was a political decision to construct a piece of valuable nature that excludes Indigenous people in what was already a highly regulated fishing area. In 2019, the International Court of Justice ruled that the British occupation was illegal, and in 2024 Britain handed over the Chagos islands, minus the island of Diego Garcia, to Mauritius, but the protected area remains in force. At the time of writing, it is unclear how this will be resolved.

Protected areas were not just established for the purpose of nature conservation. The book *Decolonizing Nature* by William M. Adams and Martin Mulligan shows how conservation allowed colonial powers to claim, control, and extract resources in designated territories. The British empire's India Forest Acts, for instance, served in the 1860s to extend colonial jurisdiction over forest resources for extraction. Later Acts included the protection of wildlife and the prohibition of Indigenous land use practices. Violence against animals outside these areas was nonetheless relentless. In the period from 1875 to 1925, more than 80,000 tigers, over 150,000 leopards, and 200,000 wolves were recorded as killed in India. The actual numbers would have been much higher as only those which were killed for bounty found their way into the record. For reference, the current tiger population in India stands at around 3,600. Early conservation legislation in Africa focused on prohibiting African use of certain agricultural and livestock management practices, such as burning, or the killing of animals with bows and arrows, which was deemed 'unmanly'. European hunters, in contrast, conducted what was described as the 'clean kills', delivered by firearm. European sporting activities, in other words, took paramountcy over Indigenous communities' livelihood practices.

Ecological degradation in the global South is commonly attributed to poor land and animal husbandry, as well as 'overpopulation', even though evidence for a direct link is often thin. Overpopulation is an old but curiously resilient idea. The 18th-century clergyman Thomas Malthus, piqued by the state resources being directed through the Poor Laws to displaced peasants in England, published in 1798 a treatise, *An Essay on the Principle of Population*, to argue that the poor should not be helped because they are 'profligate'—having too many babies without the resources/land to feed them. He contrasted the poor with the middle-class patriarch who delayed his marriage until he could afford a family. Malthus's views were popularized by people who opposed welfare support for the poor. It is no surprise that in the 1960s, when people in the global South began to aspire to a similar standard of living as the West during the process of formal decolonization, the concept of 'overpopulation' came into popular usage in the West, and always in relation to the global South. There were simply too many, they said. Geographical research by Mary Tiffen, Michael Mortimore, and Frances Gichuki in the Machakos area of Kenya debunked this argument, concluding that more people meant less erosion, due to the ability to diversify income streams and invest in beneficial land husbandry practices. Nevertheless, the popular debate on anthropogenic climate change often focuses on overpopulation rather than on the environmental impact of the wealthy. It is worth remembering that in 2023, the NGO Oxfam estimated that the world's richest 1 per cent account for more carbon emissions than the poorest 66 per cent.

More-than-human geography

Nature, we commonly assume, comprises the non-human living world, a place of untouched beauty and innocence. The less human impact on it, the more pristine it is. But understandings of nature vary tremendously from one society or culture to another. Modern Europeans have tended to see nature as external to humans, something which can be exploited for the benefit of society. This perspective has its roots in Judaeo-Christian divisions of 'Man' and 'Nature', with the former bequeathed by God the custodianship over a natural/earthly paradise, the Garden of Eden. In modernity, the idea of nature has been informed by Cartesian dualism, named after René Descartes, the 16th-century French philosopher who proposed a radical difference between mind and body. Mind, to Descartes and more broadly to the enlightenment movement, was superior to the body. As part of nature, the body lacked cognition. Whereas the mind was in the seat of rationality, the body was merely instinctual.

European ideas about the relationship between nature and society spread with European colonialism. Racialization, which placed non-European humans as lower down the evolutionary ladder and therefore closer to nature, allowed Europeans to claim superiority and custodianship of nature globally. And it was not just that colonized peoples were placed on lower stages of development, they were also constructed as more 'natural', indeed as a part of nature. It is not a coincidence that many science museums feature sections where non-Western cultures are presented to the Western eye as part of natural history. The extinction of the Thylacine, also known as the Tasmanian tiger, in the 1930s and the claim that the last aboriginal Tasmanian had died six decades earlier was followed with a similar morbid interest in European metropoles.

From a Darwinian perspective, the weak were simply
making way for the strong.

Geographers have long highlighted that any understanding of
nature has to be aided by history. This is because what we think of
as 'nature' does not have meaning outside social processes.
Critiquing the damage that market-oriented extractive activities,
including large-scale agribusiness, wreak on the environment,
Marxist geographers such as Neil Smith, Noel Castree, and Erik
Swyngedouw have grappled with the relationship between nature
and society. They argue that very little of today's world is
natural—most is the product of societal interaction with the land,
which has become more extensive under the capitalist system of
production. Even the iconic savannah landscapes that we see
today in tourist brochures are very much the product of human
activity, especially of cattle grazing by pastoralists. There is simply so
little that remains unaltered by human beings. Therefore, what we
see as nature today, especially in capitalist societies, has been
socially produced to fuel human consumption and entertainment.

In the 1980s, political ecology emerged as a subfield of both
geography and anthropology to address some of the above
questions in a fresh light. Its proponents, including Adams,
Mortimore, and Ben Wisner, were concerned with power
dynamics associated with the attribution of blame for land
degradation and the social inequalities over resource access that
were widespread in the global South, even after the ending of
formal colonialism. Such inequalities were interpreted as being
driven by development models that relied on the maintenance of
capitalist economic projects focused on the export-oriented
extraction of raw materials, mining, large-scale infrastructure
projects, or agriculture, as in the case of Indonesian and
Malaysian palm oil production.

Political ecologists recognized that some modern agricultural
methods, such as the promotion of monoculture and the use of

genetically modified seeds, that were being employed by development experts, might have improved productivity, but were causing ecological degradation and not necessarily resulting in improved standards of living for small-scale peasant farmers. Indigenous agriculture practices such as intercropping, which were deemed wasteful, were better at conserving the soil and retaining the habitats of wild animals. Yet, these practices were abandoned for the development of large-scale/industrial commercial production and because of the primacy of science, which, at the time, tended to apply knowledge generated in temperate regions to the tropics rather than constructing a dialogue between North and South.

Conservation and protected area designation and management illustrates the importance of geography or space in which conservation knowledge originates and the power dynamics affecting its implication. Feminist political ecologist Juanita Sundberg, working in Central America, encourages us to be attentive to the role that gender, often intersected with race, plays in natural resource management and the conflicts that can arise between men and women when international projects ignore local knowledge or gender roles in affected communities. In many cases, conservation may result in women losing access to land and other resources.

Recent decades have seen the rise of what is known as 'more-than-human geography', which has shown a major interest in conservation amongst other issues such as food production, gardening, and citizen science. More-than-human geographers examine how non-human animals shape encounters with humans, how they make their own worlds. The latter is known as animal agency. Its study requires immersive methodology, often ethnographic but sometimes archival, in which the researcher tries to track the animal in an attempt to understand its lived and bodily experience, to comprehend its geographies, the ways in which it reads and inscribes the landscape. Studying non-humans does not necessarily mean abandoning the kind of concepts we use to study humans. The geographer Maan Barua, for instance, uses an adapted Marxian terminology to describe animal conservation based on their value for consumers. Barua examines the role that live animals play in the accumulation of capital in the conservation mode of production, while paying crucial attention to those humans whose livelihood activities are impacted by conservation. Conservation has a price that is simultaneously pecuniary and emotional once the animal has become a commodity.

More-than-human geographers have been keen to point out the difficulty of separating out what is nature and what is society when we examine conservation practice. They are also adamant that the way in which conservation happens has a lively and unruly element which emerges from the fact that what humans are trying to manage has its own agency. One particularly fruitful case to illustrate this is the area of 'rewilding'. In response to what is seen as unfavourable transformation in the ecology of an area, conservationists have championed strategies such as the reintroduction of species and restoration ecology. The term 'rewilding' is used in a generic way to mean actions that reduce human impact or return environments to what they were like in the past. Rewilding projects are widespread. And even though there is significant variation between the global North and South, they often share in common an interest to recreate conditions in the Pleistocene, and thus before the advent of agriculture, forestry, and animal domestication.

A well-known case of rewilding has occurred in the Oostvaardersplassen (OVP), a publicly owned polder in Flevoland province of the Netherlands (Figures 16 and 17). After being reclaimed from the sea in the late 1960s, the land was originally claimed for industrial appropriation. But when these plans did not materialize, the site increasingly attracted a range of rare bird species. A few years after the 56km^2 site

16. Heck cattle and red deer at Oostvaardersplassen, 2011.

17. Map of Oostvaardersplassen, 2013.

came under public authority management, horses, cattle, and red deer were introduced. Soon, they were de-domesticated and began to contribute to the making of an ecology which some conservationists say resembles the Pleistocene. Unlike other European conservation projects, the management of the OVP was minimalist and involved no targets or models, thus introducing a dimension of unpredictability to the ways in which different species found their niche and coexisted with one another.

Of particular interest is the introduction of Heck cattle into the OVP. Heck cattle are descendants of animals which were back bred in the 1920s by two German zoologists, the Heck brothers, in an attempt to recreate the aurochs, an ancient bovine species extinct since the 17th century. The Nazi elite were interested in the Heck brothers' cows because they saw in the aurochs an authentically 'Germanic creature' whose size and aggressiveness even Julius Caesar had noted. Hermann Göring, an avid hunter and the highest-ranking Nazi to be put on trial at the 1946 Allied International Military Tribunal, had a particular passion for the idea of creating an 'über cow'. Only very few of these super cows survived the Second World War, but enough for them to be 'rewilded' at the OVP. The introduction of the herbivores was a success, their corpses creating new ecological niches for other species.

The OVP stands for a unique blend of artificial and wild dynamics. Think of the artificial land which was left to its own devices and the untameable 'back-bred' animals. The tensions between these projects challenges easy understandings of nature as something that is either out there or something that is simply produced by humans. Rewilding is not always as popular as it is in the OVP. Farmers may face the potential destruction of crops and livestock. This is the case with the reintroduction of brown bears in the Pyrenees or beavers in Scotland.

Other natures

The degree to which local communities are allowed to live and maintain their livelihoods in conservation areas has been compromised to this day, often legitimized by the claim that Indigenous peoples in particular lack the knowledge to look after the environment themselves. People of European heritage, on the other hand, have long been seen to have the expertise and the sensibilities to manage nature as well as the ability to appreciate it aesthetically.

The urgency of biodiversity loss and climate change has led some scientists and activists to embrace the concept of the Anthropocene. Challenging the universalism inherent in what Kathryn Yusoff calls 'the one humanity narrative', critics claim that not all humans bear equal responsibility. The extractive practices on which European colonialism drew relied on people of colour to do colonial capitalism's dirty work. Now it is often their descendants who live under the most immediate effects of the destruction of the planet. This has led to renewed focus on how to mitigate the effects of human actions on the environment, and especially on moving away from ecologically degrading capitalist projects.

While some scholars look at ways to construct a more sustainable capitalism, others locate the problem at a deeper level, in the Cartesian distinctions between nature and society, body and mind. They seek to transcend this modern worldview by reconsidering human–nature relationships in Western and non-Western societies and cultures. In the West, activists are advocating legal rights for natural phenomena in order to protect them from exploitation and degradation. What appears to be happening is a post-humanist turn in the West that decentres humans and instead considers how non-humans and humans are entangled in the co-production of space, much like at the OVP.

A decolonial approach seeks to understand and amplify Indigenous ontologies of human/nature relationship, by recognizing and placing Indigenous ways of being in the world on a par with those of the West. Respect for nature is widespread amongst Indigenous communities, who tend to see themselves as existing in a relational way with nature. Non-humans are understood as sentient, with selfhoods that shape their interactions with human beings. For example, in the words of Nicole Wilson and Jody Inkster:

> ...water is not just seen as a material element that makes life possible, rather for Yukon First Nations, water is a living entity, with the 'person-like' quality of agency referred to as 'spirit'... water not just enables human life by meeting physical needs, but water is life or alive—water is conceived as a living entity with metaphysical and physical properties whose well-being must be managed as with any being or subject of great importance.

This approach would involve treating non-human living beings with respect and reciprocity. When non-humans are killed, they are not killed to generate profit. Acknowledging Indigenous people's relationship with nature can be a first step to protecting nature from extractive activities carried out by outsiders, whether it be lumbering or the clearing of land for cattle ranching or mining.

Conflict with logging and mining companies, ranchers, and governments seeking to exploit their resources is often a permanent feature of Indigenous communities' lives. But sometimes they can win victories, too. In August 2023, the Ecuadorian people voted in a referendum to stop drilling in Yasuni National Park. Foregrounding this important decision is the inclusion of the Kichwa (speaking) concept of *sumak kawsay* or *Buen Vivir* (good living or well living) into the 2008 Constitution. Getting Indigenous ways of being into a country's legal system is seen as a major step in conserving the environment. While the

Ecuador example should be applauded, many governments are reliant on a development model, supported by international development agencies, in which extraction is the primary engine of economic growth. It should also be mentioned that Ecuador remains reliant on mineral and resource extraction and mining companies are still being handed contracts to exploit minerals elsewhere in the country.

In some settler colonial societies, such as New Zealand, Australia, and Canada, where Indigenous communities have ancestral claims to land, attempts have been made to introduce Indigenous ontologies into state management conservation practices. However, these are rarely successful due to ontological conflicts, clashes over what the world is made up of at its fundament. White conservationists can in many cases have difficulties understanding Indigenous worldviews and see them as something to co-opt, not something to make use of. Indigenous people are often brought into conservation as exotic objects of interest, rather than as decision-makers. Such failure amongst modern conservationists may arise from their reliance on scientific methodologies to conduct research and gather data on Indigenous knowledge. Human geographers working in this area recognize the importance of using decolonial methods that tend to be qualitative not quantitative and require collaboration and co-production with Indigenous communities. Stories, walk-alongs, local terminologies, and other citizen science methods bring new worlds and worlding practices into view. So, instead of a universal perspective on conservation that is exclusionary, market oriented, and dictated by science, human geographers recognize that Indigenous principles inform distinct approaches to environmental governance. Mutual understanding can lead to the adoption of multiple worldviews, also known as versals. With increasing biodiversity loss and the worsening impact of human-induced climate change, the need for conservation areas will persist. For human and non-living beings to coexist and thrive on planet Earth, conservation too will have to be rethought and decolonized.

Chapter 8
Beyond human geography

In this book we have sought to present something of a toolkit for how to do human geography. This has involved surveying key sub-disciplines and concepts—and seeing them applied to some of the most pressing problems of our time: social inequality, ecological crisis, and the perilous politics of the territorial state. In doing so, we hope to have shown the merits of thinking about social space on earth. But what would happen if we tried to apply human geography to the furthest reaches of the known world? What if we tried to spatialize outer space?

In late August and early September 1977, two rockets took off from Cape Canaveral in Florida, each carrying a space probe. Within years, the uncrewed *Voyager* mission would collect stunning footage from the outer margins of our solar system and send it back to earth. While *Voyager 2* is to date the only probe to have visited the 'ice giants' Uranus and Neptune, *Voyager 1* is the first human-made object to have entered interstellar space. In the hope that *Voyager* might stumble upon intelligent life, the two spacecraft carry a time capsule in the form of a golden record. The 12-inch record contains not just the location of our solar system (we can only hope that whoever finds it doesn't wish to wipe us out), but also images and recordings which were chosen to represent the entirety of 'human civilization': greetings in different languages, an image of a breastfeeding mother, and quite a lot of Johann Sebastian Bach. (The National Aeronautics and Space Administration (NASA) wanted to include 'Here comes the Sun' by *The Beatles* but their record company said no.)

Voyager is unlikely to encounter anything clever and dexterous enough to operate an LP player for a while yet. Proxima Centauri, the nearest star to our own, is more than four light years away (that's 25 trillion miles). The space probe would take about 70,000 years to get there at its current speed, were it heading in that direction. When we try to grasp these 'astronomical' scales and the seeming emptiness that opens up between celestial objects, we are confronted quite directly with the limits of our human geography. It puts planet earth in its place. Indeed, *Voyager*'s perhaps most iconic gift is the 'Pale Blue Dot' photograph. Taken in 1990 from 3.7 billion miles away, it shows our beloved blue planet as a mere dot, a pixel.

What might it mean in this context to study the human geography of outer space? Surely geography should be limited to earthly matters? After all, the *geo-* in geography is Greek for *earth* or *land*. Yes. But was it ever reasonable to study our planet in isolation from the solar system and universe? One of the founders of modern geography did not think so. Alexander von Humboldt engaged extensively in cosmography, the mapping of the heavens. But what about the *human* bit? To date, a mere 24 humans, all of whom were male US citizens, have travelled beyond low earth orbit. Unlike our own planet, what lies beyond earth orbit is untouched by human influence, a few intrepid space probes, Mars rovers, and lunar footprints notwithstanding. What on earth could there be for human geographers to think about?

Outer space can seem empty. Indeed, the distances are so vast that any comparison with earthly scales is rendered hopelessly inadequate. Unlike at sea, there is neither a legal distinction between territorial and international, nor is there an equivalent of national airspace. States do not claim territory in outer space.

But this does not mean that outer space is featureless: there is gravity and radiation, there are meteoroids and asteroids, and closer to home, quite a lot of space junk. Perhaps more importantly, outer space is hardly untouched by politics. Humans have long found ways to divide it up, similarly to how they break up planet earth into continents and regions. We speak, for instance, of earth-orbital space, interplanetary, and interstellar space. There are strategically important regions, such as the more accessible low earth orbit (below 1,200 miles) or the highly desirable geostationary orbit (at roughly 22,000 miles above the equator), at which a satellite is able to follow the earth's rotation.

While space may not be empty, it is certainly hostile, at least to the human body. Humans did not evolve to endure the temperatures common in most parts of the universe, nor its radiation levels. The lack of oxygen and low air pressure are further problems. Long periods without the earth's gravity will result in reduced bone density and chronic eye problems. Astronauts are constantly exercising to counteract the loss of muscle mass. A human lifespan, moreover, is so short, the distances in space so vast, and the speed of light such an insurmountable barrier to space travel that humanity might well be confined, in what time it has left, to the planets and moons of the solar system, most of which are really quite inhospitable.

Despite its inaccessibility, humans long gazed into the night sky to navigate the seas and contemplate the universe's deeper meaning. The stars have always attracted both scientific and spiritual modes of enquiry. There are many deities that derive their authority from a relation to cosmic forces. Astronomic discoveries too have shaped society immensely. Think about the Copernican revolution, the move from a geocentric worldview, in which the planets and the sun revolve around a stationary earth, to a heliocentric one, in which the planets circle the sun. In the late 16th century, astronomers who advocated heliocentrism were executed for questioning Christianity's earth-centric views, such was the potency of these scientific breakthroughs.

Much of human activity in space happens in low earth orbit. This is where space stations and satellites, commercial and military, are located. Our infrastructure today depends on this technology not just to function smoothly, but to function at all. The US-operated Global Positioning System (GPS) may originally have been designed to assist navigation, but it now supports a vast array of commercial, public, and military activities. Home deliveries and mobile phones are as reliant on GPS as missile warning systems and armed drones. Even the finance sector has become dependent on it. Satellite data has helped advance climate science and conservation, and aided the coordination of disaster responses, but at a significant political and environmental cost. Not only are most satellites currently in earth orbit derelict, but the rockets needed to get these up into space burn a tremendous amount of fuel. And while this currently only amounts to about 1 per cent of the fuel used in conventional aviation, rockets threaten the ozone layer and emit into the stratosphere, where they have substantial warming effects.

The Cold War space race was dominated by the United States and Soviet Union. Today, there are a number of states which have space capabilities. But this has not entailed some kind of democratization of outer space. In space too, we encounter a colonial present. Indeed, the most strategically significant regions of outer space, such as equatorial geostationary orbit, have been occupied by major spacefaring nations. Equatorial nations have not failed to notice this. In 1976, Columbia, Ecuador, Indonesia, Kenya, Uganda, and Zaire (now Democratic of Congo) signed the Bogota Declaration in an unsuccessful attempt to claim those portions of geostationary orbit which lay over their territory. Former colonies have continued to seek to develop legal tools to limit the militarization of space and to place assets in outer space under collective ownership. But to no avail. Hundreds of launch facilities across the globe take up a huge amount of land. Many are built in former European colonies because of their favourable equatorial position, which allows rockets to benefit from the earth's rotation speed.

Our cultural sphere too is saturated with colonial fantasies of space. The phrase 'space colony' is often used self-evidentially and uncritically in our media landscape. Visions of space colonization, moreover, are almost limitless and include asteroid mining, the construction of large-scale habitable infrastructure in earth orbit, the colonization and industrial exploitation of the moon and Mars, and, eventually, the expansion of the human species or forms of artificial intelligence into other solar systems and galaxies.

Arguments for space colonization typically include the following: that our planet does not host sufficient resources, that there is not enough room for pollution and waste, and, most importantly, that it is simply too small to accommodate a growing human population. Defenders of space colonization argue that the practice is unproblematic because there are no known life forms, let alone intelligent ones, in the parts of outer space that humans might be able to colonize. Unlike the case in the conquest of the Americas or the settlement of Australia, in other words, there are 'no natives'. And yet, this is a misreading of the kind of space which outer space is. Once we account for the fact that what happens in outer space really depends on terrestrial infrastructure, colonial relations of power do come into vision.

There are very significant political struggles over the often Indigenous land used for observatories and analogue habitats that simulate life off-earth. The land used for rocket launch facilities too has often to be emptied of people, which follows a familiar colonial trajectory of dispossession, extraction, and environmental degradation. Much of this happens along racial and class lines. Local economies around key space infrastructure can be surprisingly underdeveloped; the space industry has a track record of funding exploitative mining projects to quench its thirst for raw materials. Not only do rocket launches expose the local landscape to a whole range of pollutants, but global warming, which the rocket launch economy fuels, affects populations in the global South more directly than those in the global North. And it is worth noting that there are non-Western cosmologies that view space as lively, a realm not to be disturbed. To these populations, space flight will constitute a form of violence.

As the cost of launching rockets is falling, a rise in off-earth activity seems all but inevitable. There are already almost 10,000 satellites in orbit with further tens of thousands planned. One of the reasons why states have not claimed territorial sovereignty in space is the United Nations Outer Space Treaty (OST) which bans such claims. But when it was signed in 1967, the OST had not anticipated that commercial actors might one day operate in space. Companies like the Californian spacecraft manufacturer SpaceX have begun to exploit the absence of a clear legal statement on this matter. SpaceX's billionaire founder and CEO Elon Musk has pledged to colonize Mars and to create a new system of authority that ignores international law. Musk is not alone amongst ultra-rich men to delve into space tourism, asteroid mining, and space colonization. He is followed by other billionaires such as Richard Branson (Virgin Galactic) and Jeff Bezos (Blue Origin). Their declarations and rocket launches are followed by millions.

Worth $546 billion in 2022 and projected to grow by 41 per cent by 2027, the space sector is being boosted by governments. Signed by then US President Barack Obama, the 2015 Space Act has introduced legal provisions for American companies to mine asteroids for precious materials in domestic legislation. The United States has since been followed by Luxembourg, the United Arab Emirates, and Japan. In December 2022, Japan launched a rocket to the moon to collect and sell moon dust to NASA, arguably the first commercial contract for private space mining. The space tourism industry too is growing. More activity in outer space, of course, means more space junk, which is a threat to satellites and spacecraft.

Just as the Outer Space Treaty has not been able to regulate commercial actors in space, it has also struggled to contain the militarization of space. The 1991 Gulf War is sometimes thought of as the first space war because GPS was used to great effect against Saddam Hussein's forces. Since then, Washington's wars have become more rather than less dependent on space. In 2019, the United States Congress even decided to create a Space Force as a separate branch of the military. In the 2022 Ukraine war, high-resolution satellite images have had a major influence on the battlefield. Images that previously would have been restricted to military use have flooded news and social media websites, often to showcase the successful destruction of enemy units and thus garner support for the war effort. SpaceX's Starlink, a satellite internet constellation, moreover, has provided internet access to Ukrainian soldiers and civilians since the early stages of the war.

After a prolonged period in which human advances into space slowed, we are today witnessing a return of commercial and military activity. Space barons like Elon Musk can be seen as broadly perpetuating the mid-century project mapped out by settler colonial visionaries. That said, physics, money, and the needs of the human body still limit what humans can do in outer space. Life in space is unlikely to be self-sustaining. If settlements are established, they will likely look like oil platforms or research stations in Antarctica.

The fact that humans are not meaningfully inhabiting space, a few astronauts on the International Space Station notwithstanding, does not mean that the cosmos does not have a human geography. But this geography is significantly more terrestrial and mundane than the phrase 'outer space' suggests.

Extending what we have said about the analysis of social spaces in previous chapters to outer space, we are in fact going to have to think less about interstellar travel than about infrastructure and power struggles on earth: space facilities on stolen land, satellite technology that shapes how we book taxis, and rocket launches that distract us from the climate crisis on earth.

References

Chapter 1: What is human geography?

Cresswell, T. (2013) *Geographic Thought: A Critical Introduction* (Malden, Mass.: Wiley-Blackwell)

Harvey, D. (1973 [2009]) *Social Justice and the City* (Athens, Ga: University of Georgia Press)

Kropotkin, P. (1978 [1885]) 'What Geography Ought to Be', *Antipode* 10 (3): 6–15

Massey, D. (2005) *For Space* (London: Sage)

Ratzel, F. (1901 [2018]) 'Lebensraum—a Biogeographical Study. Translated by Tul'si (Tuesday) Bhambry', *Journal of Historical Geography* 61: 59–80

Semple, E. C. (1903) *American History and Its Geographic Conditions* (Boston and New York: Houghton, Mifflin and Company)

Smith, N. (1994) 'Geography, Empire and Social Theory', *Progress in Human Geography* 18: 491–500

Thrift, N. J. (2009) 'Space: The Fundamental Stuff of Geography', in N. Clifford, S. Holloway, S. Rice, and G. Valentine (eds), *Key Concepts in Geography* (London: Sage), pp. 85–96

Tuan, Y. F. (1976) 'Humanistic Geography', *Annals of the Association of American Geographers* 66 (2): 266–76

Chapter 2: The colony

Amin, S. (1988) *Eurocentrism* (New York and London: Monthly Review Press)

Blaut, J. M. (1993) *The Colonizer's Model of the World: Geographical Diffusionism and Eurocentric History* (New York: Guilford Press)

Daigle, M. and Ramirez, M. M. (2019) 'Decolonial Geographies', in Antipode Editorial Collective (eds), *Keywords in Radical Geography: Antipode at 50* (Oxford: Wiley), pp. 78–84

Gregory, D. (2004) *The Colonial Present: Afghanistan, Palestine and Iraq* (Oxford: Blackwell)

Jarosz, L. (1992) 'Constructing the Dark Continent: Metaphor as Geographic Representation of Africa', *Geografiska Annaler* 74: 105–15

Kearns, G. (2009) *Geopolitics and Empire: The Legacy of Halford Mackinder* (Oxford: Oxford University Press)

McEwan, C. (2019) *Postcolonialism, Decoloniality and Development* (London: Routledge)

Mbembe, A. (2019) *Necropolitics* (Durham, NC: Duke University Press)

Murrey, A. and Daley, P. (2023) *Learning Disobedience: Decolonizing Development Studies* (London: Pluto Books Ltd)

Rostow, W. W. (1960) *The Stages of Economic Growth: A Non-Communist Manifesto* (New York: Cambridge University Press)

Said, E. (1978) *Orientalism* (London: Penguin)

Wynter, S. (2003) 'Unsettling the Coloniality of Being/Power/Truth/ Freedom: Towards the Human, after Man, Its Overrepresentation—an Argument', *CR: The New Centennial Review* 3: 257–337

Chapter 3: The pipeline

Barry, A. (2013) *Material Politics: Disputes along the Pipeline* (Oxford: Wiley-Blackwell)

Bosworth, K. (2022) *Pipeline Populism: Grassroots Environmentalism in the Twenty-First Century* (Minneapolis: University of Minnesota Press)

Bridge, G. and Le Billon, P. (2017) *Oil* (Cambridge: Polity)

Christophers, B. (2022) 'Fossilised Capital: Price and Profit in the Energy Transition', *New Political Economy* 27: 146–59

Franta, B. (2018) 'Early Oil Industry Knowledge of CO2 and Global Warming', *Nature Climate Change* 8: 1024–5

Harvey, D. (2003) *The New Imperialism* (Oxford: Oxford University Press)

Malm, A. (2013) 'The Origins of Fossil Capital: From Water to Steam in the British Cotton Industry', *Historical Materialism* 21: 15–68

Malm, A. (2021) *How to Blow up a Pipeline* (London: Verso)

Mangat, R., Dalby, S., and Paterson, M. (2018) 'Divestment Discourse: War, Justice, Morality and Money', *Environmental Politics* 27: 187–208

Mitchell, T. (2009) 'Carbon Democracy', *Economy and Society* 38: 399–432

Murrey, A. (2015) 'Invisible Power, Visible Dispossession: The Witchcraft of a Subterranean Pipeline', *Political Geography* 47: 64–7

Rich, J. L. (1915) 'Notes on the Human Geography of an Oil Field', *Journal of Geography* 13: 185–90

Watts, M. (2012) 'The Tale of Two Gulfs: Life, Death, and Dispossession along Two Oil Frontiers', *American Quarterly* 64: 437–67

Yusoff, K. (2018) *A Billion Black Anthropocenes or None* (Minneapolis: University of Minnesota Press)

Chapter 4: The high-rise

Datta, A. and Odendaal, N. (2019) 'Smart Cities and the Banality of Power', *Environment and Planning D: Society and Space* 37: 387–92

Davis, M. (2007) *Planet of Slums* (London, New York: Verso Books)

Garmany, J. and Richmond, M. A. (2020) 'Hygienisation, Gentrification, and Urban Displacement in Brazil', *Antipode* 52: 124–44

Graham, S. (2016) *Vertical: The City from Satellites to Bunkers* (London: Verso)

Goh, K. (2018) 'Safe Cities and Queer Spaces: The Urban Politics of Radical LGBT Activism', *Annals of the American Association of Geographers* 108: 463–77

Lefebvre, H. (1996 [1968]) *Writings on Cities*, edited and translated by E. Kofman and E. Lebas (Oxford: Blackwell)

Li, Q. and Wang, L. (2022) 'Is the Chinese Skyscraper Boom Excessive?' *Journal of Urban Affairs* 44: 1117–35

Simone, A. (2004) *For the City Yet to Come: Changing African Life in Four Cities* (Durham, NC: Duke University Press)

Vasudevan, A. (2017) *The Autonomous City: A History of Urban Squatting* (London: Verso)

Chapter 5: The border

Amoore, L. (2006) 'Biometric Borders: Governing Mobilities in the War on Terror', *Political Geography* 25 (3): 336–51

Bialasiewicz, L. (2012) 'Off-shoring and Out-sourcing the Borders of EUrope: Libya and EU Border Work in the Mediterranean', *Geopolitics* 17: 843–66

Crawley, H. and Skleparis, D. (2017) 'Refugees, Migrants, Neither, Both: Categorical Fetishism and the Politics of Bounding in Europe's "Migration Crisis"', *Journal of Ethnic and Migration Studies* 44: 48–64

De Noronha, L. and Bradley, G. M. (2022) *Against Borders: The Case for Abolition* (London: New Left Books)

Elden, S. (2013) *The Birth of Territory* (Chicago: The University of Chicago Press)

Esson, J. (2020) 'Playing the Victim? Human Trafficking, African Youth, and Geographies of Structural Inequality', *Population, Space and Place* 26: e2309

Gilmore-Wilson, R. (2022) *Abolition Geographies: Essays towards Liberation* (London: Verso)

Jones, R. (2016) *Violent Borders: Refugees and the Right to Move* (London: Verso)

Kearns, G. (2017) 'The Territory of Colonialism', *Territory, Politics, Governance* 5: 222–38

Minca, C. (2015) 'Geographies of the Camp', *Political Geography* 49: 74–83

Mountz, A. (2015) 'in/Visibility and the Securitization of Migration: Shaping Publics through Border Enforcement on Islands', *Cultural Politics* 11: 184–200

Netz, R. (2003) *Barbed Wire: A Political Ecology of Modernity* (Middleton, Wis.: Wesleyan University Press)

Sack, R. D. (1983) 'Human Territoriality: A Theory', *Annals of the Association of American Geographers* 73 (1): 55–74

Vollmer, B. A. (2017) 'Security or Insecurity? Representations of the UK Border in Public and Policy Discourses', *Mobilities* 12: 295–310 (p. 295)

Chapter 6: The workplace

Crewe, L. (2017) *The Geographies of Fashion: Consumption, Space, and Value* (London and New York: Bloomsbury Academic)

Dicken, P. (2015) *Global Shift: Mapping the Contours of the Global Economy* (London: Sage)

Dutta, M. (2019) '"Becoming" Factory Workers: Understanding Women's Geographies of Work through Life Stories in Tamil Nadu, India', *Gender, Place and Culture* 26: 888–904

Fan, C. C. (2004) 'The State, the Migrant Labor Regime, and Maiden Workers in China', *Political Geography* 23: 283–305

Harvey, D. (2001) 'Globalization and the "Spatial Fix"', *Geographische Revue* 3: 23–30

Inwood, J. F. J., Brand, A. L., and Quinn, E. A. (2020) 'Racial Capital, Abolition, and a Geographic Argument for Reparations', *Antipode* 53: 1083–103

McDowell, L. (2009) *Working Bodies: Interactive Service Employment and Workplace Identities* (Oxford: Wiley)

McKittrick, K. (2011) *Demonic Grounds: Black Women and the Cartographies of Struggle* (Minneapolis: University of Minnesota Press)

Massey, D. (1984 [1995]) *Spatial Divisions of Labour: Social Structures and the Geography of Production* (New York: Methuen)

Oswin, N. (2010) 'The Modern Model Family at Home in Singapore: A Queer Geography', *Transactions of the Institute of British Geographers* 35: 256–68

Robinson, C. J. (2000) *Black Marxism: The Making of the Black Radical Tradition* (Chapel Hill, NC: University of North Carolina Press)

Strauss, K. (2020) 'Labour Geography II: Being, Knowledge and Agency', *Progress in Human Geography* 44: 150–9

Tivers, J. (1978) 'How the Other Half Lives: The Geographical Study of Women', *Area* 10: 302–6

Yeung, H. (2005) 'Rethinking Relational Economic Geography', *Transactions of the Institute of British Geographers* 30: 37–51

Chapter 7: The conservation area

Adams, W. M. (2020) 'Geographies of Conservation III: Nature's Spaces', *Progress in Human Geography* 44: 789–801

Barua, M. (2016) 'Lively Commodities and Encounter Value', *Environment and Planning D* 34: 1462–78

Brockington, D. (2002) *Fortress Conservation: The Preservation of the Mkomazi Game Reserve, Tanzania* (Oxford: James Currey)

Brockington, D. and Scholfield, K. (2010) 'The Conservationist Mode of Production and Conservation NGOs in Sub-Saharan Africa', *Antipode* 42: 551–75

Castree, N. (2017) 'The Production of Nature', in E. Sheppard and T. Barnes (eds), *A Companion to Economic Geography* (Hoboken, NJ: Wiley Online), pp. 275–89

De Santo, E. M., Jones, P. J. S., and Miller, A. M. M. (2011) 'Fortress Conservation at Sea: A Commentary on the Chagos Marine Protected Area', *Marine Policy* 35 (2): 258–60

Koot, S., Büscher, B., and Thakholi, L. (2024) 'The New Green Apartheid? Race, Capital and Logics of Enclosure in South Africa's Wildlife Economy', *Environment and Planning E: Nature and Space* 7 (1): 123–40

Lorimer, J. and Driessen, C. (2014) 'Wild Experiments at the Oostvaardersplassen', *Transactions of the Institute of British Geographers* 39: 169–81

Radcliffe, S. A. (2012) 'Development for the Post-Neoliberal Era? *Sumak Kawsay*, Living Well and the Limits to Decolonization in Ecuador', *Geoforum* 43: 240–9

Saldanha, A. (2020) 'A Date with Destiny: Racial Capitalism and the Beginnings of the Anthropocene', *Environment and Planning D* 38: 12–34

Smith, N. (2010) *Uneven Development: Nature, Capital, and the Production of Space* (3rd edition, London: Verso)

Sundberg, J. (2004) 'Identities in the Making: Conservation, Gender and Race in the Maya Biosphere Reserve, Guatemala', *Gender, Place & Culture* 11 (1): 43–66

Swyngedouw, E. (2018) 'The Urbanization of Capital and the Production of Capitalist Natures', in M. Vidal et al. (eds), *The Oxford Handbook of Karl Marx* (Oxford: Oxford University Press), pp. 539–56

Tiffen, M., Mortimore, M. J., and Gichuki, F. (1994) *More People, Less Erosion: Environmental Recovery in Kenya* (Chichester: John Wiley)

Wilson, N. J. and Inkster, J. (2018) 'Respecting Water: Indigenous Water Governance, Ontologies, and the Politics of Kinship on the Ground', *Environment and Planning E* 1: 516–38

Wisner, B. (2015) 'Speaking Truth to Power: A personal account of activist political ecology', in Tom Perreault, Gavin Bridge, and James McCarthy (eds), *The Routledge Handbook of Political Ecology* (London and New York: Routledge), pp. 53–63

Chapter 8: Beyond human geography

Deudney, D. (2020) *Dark Skies: Space Expansionism, Planetary Geopolitics, and the Ends of Humanity* (New York: Oxford University Press)

Dodds, K. (2021) *Border Wars: The Conflicts that Will Define Our Future* (London: Ebury)

Klinger, J. M. (2021) 'Environmental Geopolitics and Outer Space', *Geopolitics* 26: 666–703

Sammler, K. G. and Lynch, C. R. (2021) 'Apparatuses of Observation: Settler Colonialism and Space Science in Hawai'i', *Environment and Planning D* 39: 945–65

Index

GEOGRAPHY
A Very Short Introduction
John A. Matthews & David T. Herbert

Modern Geography has come a long way from its historical roots in exploring foreign lands, and simply mapping and naming the regions of the world. Spanning both physical and human Geography, the discipline today is unique as a subject which can bridge the divide between the sciences and the humanities, and between the environment and our society. Using wide-ranging examples from global warming and oil, to urbanization and ethnicity, this *Very Short Introduction* paints a broad picture of the current state of Geography, its subject matter, concepts and methods, and its strengths and controversies. The book's conclusion is no less than a manifesto for Geography' future.

> 'Matthews and Herbert's book is written- as befits the VSI series- in an accessible prose style and is peppered with attractive and understandable images, graphs and tables.'
>
> **Geographical.**

www.oup.com/vsi

GEOPOLITICS
A Very Short Introduction
Klaus Dodds

In certain places such as Iraq or Lebanon, moving a few feet either side of a territorial boundary can be a matter of life or death, dramatically highlighting the connections between place and politics. For a country's location and size as well as its sovereignty and resources all affect how the people that live there understand and interact with the wider world. Using wide-ranging examples, from historical maps to James Bond films and the rhetoric of political leaders like Churchill and George W. Bush, this Very Short Introduction shows why, for a full understanding of contemporary global politics, it is not just smart - it is essential - to be geopolitical.

'Engrossing study of a complex topic.'

Mick Herron, Geographical.

GLOBALIZATION
A Very Short Introduction
Manfred Steger

'Globalization' has become one of the defining buzzwords of our time - a term that describes a variety of accelerating economic, political, cultural, ideological, and environmental processes that are rapidly altering our experience of the world. It is by its nature a dynamic topic - and this *Very Short Introduction* has been fully updated for 2009, to include developments in global politics, the impact of terrorism, and environmental issues. Presenting globalization in accessible language as a multifaceted process encompassing global, regional, and local aspects of social life, Manfred B. Steger looks at its causes and effects, examines whether it is a new phenomenon, and explores the question of whether, ultimately, globalization is a good or a bad thing.

www.oup.com/vsi

LANDSCAPES AND GEOMORPHOLOGY
A Very Short Introduction
Andrew Goudie & Heather Viles

Landscapes are all around us, but most of us know very little about how they have developed, what goes on in them, and how they react to changing climates, tectonics and human activities. Examining what landscape is, and how we use a range of ideas and techniques to study it, Andrew Goudie and Heather Viles demonstrate how geomorphologists have built on classic methods pioneered by some great 19th century scientists to examine our Earth. Using examples from around the world, including New Zealand, the Tibetan Plateau, and the deserts of the Middle East, they examine some of the key controls on landscape today such as tectonics and climate, as well as humans and the living world.

www.oup.com/vsi

INTERNATIONAL MIGRATION
A Very Short Introduction
Khalid Koser

Why has international migration become an issue of such intense public and political concern? How closely linked are migrants with terrorist organizations? What factors lie behind the dramatic increase in the number of women migrating? This *Very Short Introduction* examines the phenomenon of international human migration - both legal and illegal. Taking a global look at politics, economics, and globalization, the author presents the human side of topics such as asylum and refugees, human trafficking, migrant smuggling, development, and the international labour force.

www.oup.com/vsi

ENVIRONMENTAL LAW

A Very Short Introduction

Elizabeth Fisher

Environmental law is the law concerned with environmental problems. It is a vast area of law that operates from the local to the global, involving a range of different legal and regulatory techniques. In theory, environmental protection is a no brainer. Few people would actively argue for pollution or environmental destruction. Ensuring a clean environment is ethically desirable, and also sensible from a purely self-interested perspective. Yet, in practice, environmental law is a messy and complex business fraught with conflict. Whilst environmental law is often characterized in overly simplistic terms, with a law being seen as be a simple solution to environmental problems, the reality is that creating and maintaining a body of laws to address and avoid problems is not easy, and involves legislators, courts, regulators, and communities.

This *Very Short Introduction* provides an overview of the main features of environmental law, and discusses how environmental law deals with multiple interests, socio-political conflicts, and the limits of knowledge about the environment. Showing how interdependent societies across the world have developed robust and legitimate bodies of law to address environmental problems, Elizabeth Fisher discusses some of the major issues and controversies involved in environmental law.

www.oup.com/vsi

GLOBAL ECONOMIC HISTORY
A Very Short Introduction
Robert C. Allen

Why are some countries rich and others poor? In 1500, the income differences were small, but they have grown dramatically since Columbus reached America. Since then, the interplay between geography, globalization, technological change, and economic policy has determined the wealth and poverty of nations. The industrial revolution was Britain's path breaking response to the challenge of globalization. Western Europe and North America joined Britain to form a club of rich nations by pursuing four polices: creating a national market by abolishing internal tariffs and investing in transportation, erecting an external tariff to protect their fledgling industries from British competition, banks to stabilize the currency and mobilize domestic savings for investment, and mass education to prepare people for industrial work.

Together these countries pioneered new technologies that have made them ever richer. Before the Industrial Revolution, most of the world's manufacturing was done in Asia, but industries from Casablanca to Canton were destroyed by western competition in the nineteenth century, and Asia was transformed into 'underdeveloped countries' specializing in agriculture. The spread of economic development has been slow since modern technology was invented to fit the needs of rich countries and is ill adapted to the economic and geographical conditions of poor countries. A few countries—Japan, Soviet Russia, South Korea, Taiwan, and perhaps China—have, nonetheless, caught up with the West through creative responses to the technological challenge and with Big Push industrialization that has achieved rapid growth through investment coordination. Whether other countries can emulate the success of East Asia is a challenge for the future.

www.oup.com/vsi

DEVELOPMENT
A Very Short Introduction
Ian Goldin

What do we mean by development? How can citizens, governments, and the international community foster development?

The process by which nations escape poverty and achieve economic and social progress has been the subject of extensive examination for hundreds of years. The notion of development itself has evolved from an original preoccupation with incomes and economic growth to a much broader understanding of development.

In this *Very Short Introduction* Ian Goldin considers the contributions that education, health, gender, equity, and other dimensions of human well-being make to development, and discusses why it is also necessary to include the role of institutions and the rule of law as well as sustainability and environmental concerns.

2 0 4